William Arnold Stevens, Alvah Hovey, Ezra Palmer Gould

Commentary on the epistle to the Galatians

William Arnold Stevens, Alvah Hovey, Ezra Palmer Gould

Commentary on the epistle to the Galatians

ISBN/EAN: 9783337731038

Printed in Europe, USA, Canada, Australia, Japan

Cover: Foto ©Lupo / pixelio.de

More available books at **www.hansebooks.com**

AN

AMERICAN COMMENTARY

ON THE

NEW TESTAMENT.

EDITED BY

ALVAH HOVEY, D.D., LL.D.

PHILADELPHIA.
AMERICAN BAPTIST PUBLICATION SOCIETY,
1420 CHESTNUT STREET.

ON THE

EPISTLE TO THE GALATIANS.

BY
ALVAH HOVEY, D. D., LL.D.

PHILADELPHIA:
AMERICAN BAPTIST PUBLICATION SOCIETY,
1420 CHESTNUT STREET.

INTRODUCTION TO THE EPISTLE TO THE GALATIANS.

There are a few general questions in respect to such a writing as the Epistle to the Galatians which should be answered, if possible, before attempting an explanation of its language, paragraph by paragraph, and verse by verse. They relate to the writer, the readers, the occasion, the structure, and the date of the Epistle, together with the influence which it has had upon Christian doctrine and life, and the use which has been made of it in modern controversy. Correct answers to these questions will lighten the interpreter's work, and render it more useful to the reader.

I. THE WRITER.

This Epistle purports to have been written by the Apostle Paul (1 : 1), and it is numbered by Eusebius among his undisputed writings. "The epistles of Paul are fourteen, all well known and beyond doubt. It should not, however, be concealed that some have set aside the Epistle to the Hebrews, saying that it was disputed as not being one of Paul's epistles." ("Hist. Eccl.," III. 3.) This statement deserves full confidence, for Eusebius was acquainted with a considerable body of Christian literature produced in the first three centuries, and current at the beginning of the fourth, but since lost, and his account of the estimate which had been put upon the several books of the New Testament, down to his own time, has never been successfully impeached.

His statement is also confirmed by the earliest versions, for this Epistle is found, in connection with the other epistles of Paul, in the Syriac and Old Latin Versions which are assigned to the Second Century, and in the Egyptian, which was probably completed before the middle of the Third. It is clearly recognized in the Muratorian Canon not later than A. D. 170, and is contained in all the early manuscripts of the epistles of Paul. (E. g., א A B C D E F G.)

The statement of Eusebius is still further confirmed by the language of Irenæus "Against Heresies" (III. 13 : 3 ; 6 : 5 ; 7 : 2 ; 16 : 7 ; 21 : 1 ; 22 : 1 ; V. 3 : 5 ; 11 : 1 ; 21 : 1 ; 32 : 2), according to the old Latin translation, which is, of course, less decisive than the original Greek would have been ; by the argument of Tertullian, in his treatise "Against Marcion" (V. 2–4), which attributes the Epistle to Paul, and reasons from it as if it were accepted by Marcion, who rejected many books of the New Testament ; by quotations from it in the writings of Clement of Alexandria ("The Pedagogue," I. 6, 11, and "Stromata," III. 15), who sometimes mentions the name of Paul, and, at others, calls him simply "the apostle"; and by the words of Origen (e. g., on Rom. 3 : 27, 29), as translated by Rufinus. Jerome says that Origen "wrote five volumes on the Epistle of Paul to the Galatians," but only three fragments of this commentary have been preserved in a Latin translation.

5

Having such evidence of its genuineness, we need not appeal to traces of an acquaintance with this Epistle on the part of the Apostolical Fathers, who do not specify the New Testament books from which they quote. Yet their writings furnish a degree of proof, not altogether unwelcome, that this Epistle was extant at the beginning of the Second Century. (See Clement of Rome *ad* Corinth. 3 : 1 ; Ignatius *ad* Polyc. 1 ; Polycarp *ad* Phil. cc. 3, 5, 6, 12.)

It is well known that the Epistle to the Galatians is one of the four which were recognized by F. C. Baur as genuine, and that the principal writers of his school have agreed with their master in this respect. To say nothing of other reasons for their opinion, it must be admitted that the character of these four epistles affords the clearest evidence of their genuineness, for they are intensely real and practical. "They deal with specific evils ; they refute definite errors ; they repel particular slanders ; they check given disorders ; they assert special rights ; they prescribe rules for the treatment of distinct offenses. Sharp logic, open rebuke, fervid appeal, generous praise, follow one another in quick succession. What love to those addressed glows in the writer's language ! What readiness to be spent in their service ! What downright honesty, fidelity, and greatness of soul breathe in every page ! These sentences were called forth by the wants of living men, or we may close up the volume of history. Whoever can look upon them as spurious, must have lost the sense of reality, the power of distinguishing between the actual and the ideal, and may well despair of finding anything trustworthy in all the records of the past." (Quoted from the author's sermon in "Madison Avenue Lectures.") It is incredible that either of these letters was written by any other man than the Apostle Paul.

II. THE READERS.

The churches addressed by Paul in this Epistle were located in Galatia, a middle province of Asia Minor, one third larger than Palestine west of the Jordan, and inhabited by a mixed population of Phrygians, Gauls, Greeks, Jews, and Romans. Speaking in a general way, the Romans were there as civil or military officers, with their attendants and soldiers, and naturally formed a class by themselves, superior to the rest of the people, and distinct from them in social life. The Jews were there, as in all parts of Asia Minor, for traffic ; and, to accomplish the purpose of their foreign residence, they must have mingled in business with men of every class. The Greeks also were there for a somewhat similar purpose, and in such numbers that their language became the medium of general intercourse, being understood by all the more intelligent people. But all these were, nevertheless, to a certain degree foreigners. On the other hand, the Phrygians were the original possessors of the land, yet, since B. C. 241, if not 279, a period of not less than three centuries, they had been a subject race in Galatia, less influential, and perhaps less numerous, than the Gauls ; for the latter, a restless swarm from the full Celtic hive of Western Europe, had given their name to the province conquered by them, and, it is believed, had also imparted somewhat of their special temperament to the Christian churches founded among them by Paul.

"Galatia," says Lightfoot, "was parceled out among the three tribes of which the invading Gauls were composed in the following way : the Troemi occupied the easternmost portion, bordering on Cappadocia and Pontus, with Tavium, or Tavia, as their chief town ; the Tolistobogii, who were situated to the west, on the frontier of Bithynia and Phrygia-Epictetus, fixed upon the ancient Pessinus for their capital ; the Tectosages settled in the centre, between the other two tribes, adopting Ancyra as their seat of government, regarded also as the metropolis of the whole of Galatia." All these tribes were subjugated to the Roman power by the Consul Manlius in 189 B. C., and the whole territory was made a Roman province by Augustus in 25 B. C. This was its civil status when visited by Paul, three quarters of a century later, the Eastern Gauls having learned, with their Western kinsmen, the futility of resisting the might of Imperial Rome.

But what were the characteristics of the Celtic race, as described by classic writers? And how do they agree with the traits which appear to have distinguished the Galatian Christians addressed by Paul? The Roman and Greek writers speak of the Celts, or Gauls, as men of large stature, white skin, blue eyes, and light-colored hair. They refer to their ingenuity and versatile talent; to their warlike spirit and desperate courage; to their restless activity and predatory life. But they accuse them of fickleness, intemperance, and superstition. Yet a competent modern scholar affirms that "a braver set of men never faced the enemy than the Galli with whom Cæsar fought. Most of them were children of poverty, brought up to suffer and to die. We often read, at earlier periods, of their losing, through intemperance, the fruits of a hard-fought battle; but nothing of this kind appears in the Gallic wars." (George Love, in "Dict. of Gr. and Rom. Geog.," page 964.) Cæsar remarks that they were "a nation greatly given to superstitions" (*religionibus*). And it will hardly be denied that, as a race, they were ardent, impulsive, and brave, but at the same time rash, unstable, and, perhaps, volatile. This description, drawn from classic sources, accords in a very striking manner with the suggestions of the Epistle to the Galatians as to the character of the persons who received that Epistle.

But it may be presumed that some of those addressed were of Phrygian descent, and the question may be asked, What sort of men were the Phrygians? As previously stated, they appear to have been the earliest inhabitants of Central Asia Minor. "Their disposition was peaceable. No one of their traditions or legends points to a heroic period in their history, but all have a somewhat mystic or fantastic character. Agriculture was their chief occupation, and they never took or exacted an oath. Their proper divinities were Cybele and Dionysus, called by them Sabazius. With the worship of these deities were connected the celebrated orgiastic rites, accompanied by wild music and dances, which were subsequently introduced among the Greeks. All that we hear of the religion of the Phrygians during the historical times appears to show that it was a mixture of their own original form of worship with the less pure rites introduced by the Syro-Phœnician tribes." (Quoted freely from Leonhard Schmitz, in "Dict. of Gr. and Rom. Geog.," II., page 623.) It may then be conjectured, from all that is known of the mixed population of Galatia, that the churches founded by Paul were composed chiefly of persons of Gallic or Phrygian descent, the former being far more influential than the latter, while there was in all of them a small fraction of Greeks, Jews, and possibly Romans.

III. THE OCCASION.

In his second missionary journey (A. D. 51 or 52) Paul preached Christ for the first time in Galatia. (Acts 16 : 6.) The people received the apostle with great kindness and respect (Gal. 4 : 13, 14), many of them becoming followers of the Lord Jesus. About three years later (i. e., in the autumn of A. D. 54, or early in A. D. 55), he revisited the churches of this province (Acts 18 : 27), and was led by what he saw to warn them in strong language against perversions of the gospel which he had preached to them (Gal. 1 : 9.) Already, therefore, it may be presumed, had Judaistic doctrines been broached among them, and listened to with some degree of favor. But the apostle's urgent protest against those doctrines seemed to be effectual, and he left them, doubtless, with the feeling that any danger to their faith had been averted.

Yet he was mistaken. The Judaizing zealots ere long resumed their efforts, asserting that Gentiles could not be saved without being circumcised and obeying the law. Their influence was so great that, within a comparatively short time (Gal. 1 : 6), many were almost persuaded to submit to the rite of circumcision. They must have impugned the apostolic authority of Paul, partly by laying stress on the fact that he had never been taught by Christ himself, but had obtained his knowledge of the gospel at second hand, and partly by saying that his doctrine was different from that of Peter and James, who observed the Jewish law.

How many adversaries of Paul appeared in the Galatian churches, it is impossible to ascertain ; but it is safe to conclude that they were Jewish Christians, rather than simply Jews, for the latter would have urged the Galatians to renounce Christ and obey Moses, instead of teaching them to supplement the gospel with the law. We may also assume that this movement did not spring from the churches themselves, but that it came to them from abroad, and perhaps from Palestine. Compare Acts 15 : 1 ; Gal. 2 : 12.

But whether these perverters of the gospel were few or many, were from Palestine or some other place, they were so plausible in their criticism of Paul's authority as an apostle, or so persuasive in their reasoning for obedience to the law as a condition of acceptance with God, or so earnest and urgent in their assertions and appeals, that their Celtic hearers were greatly moved, and on the point of yielding submission to the new doctrine. This was the emergency which called for the Epistle to the Galatians, and with assertion most direct, and argument most powerful, and appeal most tender, did the apostle meet the emergency.

IV. THE STRUCTURE.

This was evidently determined by the object to be accomplished, and, viewed in that light, it is perfectly logical and clear. Indeed, it would be difficult to find anywhere a better specimen of cogent and persuasive writing. The first two chapters assert and establish Paul's claim to a knowledge of Christian truth as original and complete as that of the earlier apostles. It had been received by him from Christ by direct revelation, and it comprised all the facts and principles essential to the gospel of the grace of God.

The next two chapters verify the truth and sufficiency of that gospel by an appeal to the experience of his readers when and since they received it, by an exposition of the way of life according to the ancient Scriptures, and by a statement of the relation of the law of God to his promise, of Mosaic legalism to justification through faith in Christ.

And the last two chapters warn the Galatians against any misapprehension or abuse of his doctrine by explaining the operation of faith and exhorting them to a holy life in the freedom which belongs to sons of God.

A fuller and beautiful analysis of the apostle's course of thought is quoted, in connection with the successive paragraphs of the Epistle, from an article by Dr. Hackett in the "Christian Review" for October, 1861, pages 577–584.

V. THE DATE.

This may be placed without hesitation after Paul's second visit to Galatia, on his third missionary journey (Acts 18 : 23), and either during his residence of more than two years in Ephesus (Acts 19 : 8, 10, 22), or his visit to Macedonia and Corinth thereafter. (Acts 20 : 1–3.) In this period the most interesting group of his epistles was written; namely, those sent to the Corinthians, Galatians, and Romans. And the question to be answered is this : Was the Epistle to the Galatians written in the first part of his residence in Ephesus, or during his visit to Macedonia and Corinth? Was it written before the two Epistles to the Corinthians, or after them? For careful interpreters agree that the Epistle to the Romans was probably written later than any other belonging to this group.

The principal argument for dating it in the early part of his sojourn at Ephesus is drawn from Gal. 1 : 6—"I marvel that ye are so soon removing from him that called you in the grace of Jesus Christ unto another gospel"—for "so soon" (οὕτως ταχέως) is thought to imply that only a short time had passed since his last visit to them, or, possibly, since their conversion. A change taking place after three years would not have been thus characterized. Indeed, most of those who rely on this argument believe that only a few months could have elapsed between the earlier events which the apostle has in mind and the change in the state of the churches which called forth his letter—i. e., between his last visit to them and the letter he was writing.

But the inference from these words seems to me precarious. (1) Because the *terminus a quo* is by no means certain. It may have been the time when the Judaizing teachers began, or resumed, their efforts to shake the confidence of the Galatians in the apostle and his gospel. If anything in the context forbids this, it must be the words, "from him that called you in the grace of Jesus Christ," which refer to their conversion more than three years (if not six) previous to his writing this Epistle. But Paul's reference to their conversion, as a work of God's grace in Christ Jesus, agrees with the whole strain of argument in the Epistle, and can easily be accounted for without assuming that it was the date from which he reckoned in using the words "so soon." (2) Because, as Lightfoot remarks, "it is possible that 'soon' (ταχέως) here may signify 'readily, rashly,' that is, 'quickly' after the opportunity is offered, a sense which the present tense, *are turning renegades* (μετα-τίθεσθε), would facilitate. See 1 Tim. 5 : 22 ; 2 Thess. 2 : 2. In this case there will be no reference to any independent point of time." The sole reference would be to the quickness or rapidity of the change. Hence the argument from ταχέως is untrustworthy.

But the reasons for thinking that this Epistle was written a short time before the Epistle to the Romans appear to me of real weight. And the most important of these is the remarkable coincidence of thought and expression in many passages of the two letters. The following instances of similarity are adduced by Lightfoot in his Introduction to this Epistle : (1) Gal. 3 : 6=Rom. 4 : 3 ; Gal. 3 : 7=Rom. 4 : 10, 11 ; Gal. 3 : 8=Rom. 4 : 17 ; Gal. 3 : 9=Rom. 4 : 23 ; Gal. 3 : 10=Rom. 4 : 15 ; Gal. 3 : 11=Rom. 3 : 21, seq. ; Gal. 3 : 12= Rom. 10 : 5 ; Gal. 3 : 13, 14=Rom. 4 : 23, 24 ; Gal. 3 : 15–18=Rom. 4 : 13, 14, 16 ; Gal. 3 : 19–21=Rom. 7 : 1–3 ; Gal. 3 : 22=Rom. 11 : 32 ; 3 : 9, 10 ; Gal. 3 : 23–26=Rom. 7 : 1–3 ; Gal. 3 : 27=Rom. 6 : 3 ; 13 : 14 ; Gal. 3 : 29=Rom. 9 : 8 ; Gal. 4 : 5, 6, 7= Rom. 8 : 14–17. (2) Gal. 2 : 16=Rom. 3 : 20. (3) Gal. 2 : 19=Rom. 7 : 4, cf. 6 : 2–5 ; Gal. 2 : 20 (cf. 5 : 24 ; 6 : 14)=Rom. 6 : 6, 8, 11. (4) Gal. 4 : 23, 28=Rom. 9 : 7, 8. (5) Gal. 5 : 14=Rom. 13 : 8, 9, 10. (6) Gal. 5 : 16=Rom. 8 : 4 ; Gal. 5 : 17=Rom. 7 : 23, 25 ; Gal. 5 : 17=Rom. 7 : 15 ; Gal. 5 : 18=Rom. 8 : 2. (7) Gal. 6 : 2=Rom. 15 : 1. These parallels render it extremely probable that the two epistles were written about the same time, or within two or three months of each other.

And it is no less evident that the Epistle to the Galatians was written before, rather than after, the Epistle to the Romans, for the former reads like a first draft, and not like a condensation of the latter. The ampler and calmer unfolding of doctrine in the Epistle to the Romans agrees with all the circumstances of the case, if we assume : (1) that the Epistle to the Galatians was written under the excitement of intense anxiety occasioned by a sudden and dangerous crisis in the churches addressed ; (2) that those churches were saved from apostasy, and fixed in their adhesion to Christ as the only Saviour, by means of this letter ; and (3) that, two or three months later, relieved of his extreme anxiety concerning the church at Corinth and the churches of Galatia, yet sensible of the unwearied activity of the Judaizing party, and wishing to forestall its work in Rome, he wrote the greatest of his epistles to the Christians of that city, and set forth in it with elaborate care, on the lines which he had sketched in his earlier epistle, the gospel of the grace of God through the death of Christ for the sins of men.

It seems probable, therefore, that the Epistle to the Galatians was written early in A. D. 58, soon after Paul's arrival in Corinth, or while he was on his way to that city.

VI. USE AND MISUSE.

As students of the German Reformation are aware, Martin Luther prized this Epistle very highly, and commented on it frequently. In it he discovered the marrow of the gospel : the doctrine of justification through faith in Christ. "It is very necessary," he wrote, "that this doctrine be kept in continual practice and public exercise, both of reading and hearing. It can never be taught, urged, and repeated enough. If this doctrine be lost, then is also the doctrine of truth, life, and salvation, lost and gone. If this doctrine flourishes, then all good things flourish ; religion, the true service of God, the glory of God, the right knowledge of all things which are necessary for a Christian man to know." (Preface, page 130.) The Epistle to the Galatians has been one of the clearest sources of evangelical truth since the Bible was put in the hands of the people.

But it has also been compelled to serve those who deny the divine origin of the gospel which it teaches. "The earliest form of Christianity," it is argued, "was a modified Judaism. The distinctive features of the system current under this name were added by St. Paul. There was an irreconcileable opposition between the apostle of the Gentiles and the apostles of the Jews—a personal feud between the teachers themselves, and a direct antagonism between their doctrines. After a long struggle, St. Paul prevailed, and Christianity—our Christianity—was the result." (Lightfoot, Introduction, page 66.) An impartial study of the Epistle will, however, lead to a different conclusion—a conclusion that the account which Paul gives of his relation to the other apostles is worthy of entire confidence. And, if so, there was no personal feud between the apostles, and no radical difference between them as to the true way of life through Christ, but, on the contrary, a full recognition, after suitable proof, of Paul's apostolic mission and doctrine, on the part of James, Peter, and John, together with an amicable division of the work of evangelization between them and him. To build upon this Epistle such a theory as that of Baur is, therefore, I am persuaded, a misuse of its language which will not bear the test of unbiased criticism.

Note.—Among the works consulted with profit in the preparation of this commentary, besides the grammars of Winer and Buttmann, are the commentaries of Lightfoot, Ellicott, Jowett, Howson, Sanday, Schaff, Beet, and Luther (translated) in English, with those of Sieffert-Meyer, Rückert, De Wette, and Wieseler in German, and those of Calvin and Bengel in Latin, while, in studying some of the doctrinal passages, the works of Usteri ("Der Paulinische Lehrbegriff"), Messner ("Die Theologie der Apostel"), and Weiss ("Theology of the New Testament"), have been examined. The writer is also greatly indebted to his former teacher, Dr. H. B. Hackett, not only for the Analysis which he published first in the "Bibliotheca Sacra," and later, with additions, in the "Christian Review" for 1861, 577–584, but also for his articles in the "Bibliotheca Sacra," XIX., 211–225, and XXII., 138–149, on the translation of several passages of the Epistle, and for the eloquent oral exposition of the whole Epistle which he gave to the class of 1848 in the Newton Theological Institution, as preserved in notes and a paraphrase written at the time.

THE EPISTLE TO THE GALATIANS.

CHAPTER I.

PAUL, an apostle, (not of men, neither by man, but by Jesus Christ, and God the Father, who raised him from the dead;)

1 Paul, an apostle (not from men, neither through ¹ man, but through Jesus Christ, and God the Father,

1 Or, *a man.*

Ch. 1 : 1-5 : ADDRESS AND GREETING.— "In the introduction," says Dr. Hackett, "Paul asserts in the strongest manner the divine origin of his apostleship, and his appointment to it without any human intervention; and invokes on the Galatians the usual benediction from God the Father and the Lord Jesus Christ. In this connection he brings incidentally into view the sacrifice and death of Christ as the means of human salvation, and thus announces the great theme of the Epistle at the outset. (1 : 1-5.)" See "Christian Review" for 1861, page 578.

1. Paul—called Saul in the earlier chapters of the Acts. (7:58; 8:1; 9:1,4,8.) The name 'Paul' appears for the first time in Acts 13 : 9, after the apostle had entered upon his distinctive missionary work among the Gentiles. Saul is a Hebrew, and Paul a Roman name. The meaning of the former is *asked for*, and the meaning of the latter *little*. The resemblance in sound must be considered accidental. Probably both names were given him in childhood, as by descent he was a Jew or Hebrew (Phil. 3 : 5), and in civil standing a Roman. (Acts 16 : 37; 22 : 25-28.) **Apostle**—used here in the highest Christian sense of the word to denote one specially commissioned to preach the gospel. The apostles held the first place under Christ in his kingdom. See 1 Cor. 12 : 28, seq. ; Eph. 4 : 11. In addressing his epistles to the Thessalonians, Paul had made no reference to his apostleship, doubtless because it was admitted without question by them; but now, writing to churches in which his equality with the original apostles had evidently been denied, he asserts it promptly and positively at the outset, and in his later epistles he does the same thing with more or less emphasis. **Not of** (or, *from*) **men.** These words deny that his commission was of human origin. This denial may have been called forth by the insinuations of Judaizing teachers, who had

appeared in Galatia, that his authority was derived from men, perhaps from the church at Antioch. **Neither by man** (or, *nor through a man*). By this added clause Paul denies that any man had been the medium or channel through which his commission to serve as an apostle had been made known to him. It was in no sense or degree human. Doubtless it had been urged in favor of the higher dignity of the earlier apostles that they had been commissioned by the lips of Christ himself, while Paul must have received his commission through some one who was a disciple before him. **But by** (*through*) **Jesus Christ**—who had appeared to him on the way to Damascus (Acts 9 : 3, seq.; 26 : 16-18), and had pointed out at that early day the special work which he was to perform. Even if we suppose that, according to Luke's narrative in Acts 9 : 3, seq., Jesus Christ made use of Ananias as his mouthpiece, the words of Christ to Paul rendered the language of Ananias virtually Christ's language, and the apostle was therefore justified in treating it as such, overlooking the human agency. **And God the Father** —that is, his apostolic commission was conveyed through Jesus Christ, who is inseparably united in action with God the Father, so that Christ's action is really his Father's action as well. In this case, at least, what Jesus did the Father did. The expression 'Father' is best understood as meaning here the Father of Jesus Christ. **Who raised him from the dead.** This seems to have been added because it was not during his earthly life that Jesus appeared to Paul and made him an apostle; it was rather after his resurrection and ascension. And that resurrection was the work of his Father, though not in such a sense as to exclude his own participation in it. The meaning of the Greek expression, translated 'from the dead' (ἐκ νεκρῶν), is explained by Winer("Grammar," p. 123), as follows: "'the

13

2 And all the brethren which are with me, unto the churches of Galatia:
3 Grace *be* to you, and peace, from God the Father, and *from* our Lord Jesus Christ,
4 Who gave himself for our sins, that he might deliver us from this present evil world, according to the will of God and our Father:

2 who raised him from the dead), and all the brethren who are with me, unto the churches of Galatia:
3 Grace to you and peace [1]from God the Father, and our Lord Jesus Christ, who gave himself for our sins, that he might deliver us out of this present evil [2]world, according to the will of [3]our God

---

1 Some ancient authorities read *from God our Father, and the Lord Jesus Christ*......2 Or, *age*......3 Or, *God and our Father*.

---

dead' appears to signify 'the assembly of the dead.'" See also Thayer's "Lexicon of the New Testament," on the word νεκρός.

2. And all the brethren which (*that*) **are with me.** This does not mean all the members of the church where he was, or all the Christians that happened to be present with Paul when he indited this letter, but rather 'all the brethren who are at present my companions in travel and preaching.' Thus, when writing to the Thessalonians, he associated with himself Silvanus and Timothy in his salutation to the church. In the present case he forbears to give the names of his associates in labor, though he must have communicated to them his purpose of writing the letter, and very likely the substance of the letter itself. **Unto the churches of Galatia**—that is, the churches located somewhere in the province of Galatia. It may be inferred that they were not all in one city, but were independent bodies found in different places. None of them can be positively assigned to particular cities, as Ancyra, Pessinus, or Tavium.

The entire absence of commendation in this address is worthy of notice. The Christians to whom he writes are simply 'churches.' He can pray for them, but he is now in no mood to praise them. Deeply agitated by what he has heard of their fickleness and inclination to Judaism, he has no heart to speak in this place of the evidences of divine life in those to whom he writes.

3. Grace be to you, and peace. 'Grace' is unmerited favor, and when it is God's favor its natural result is 'peace.' **From God the Father.** According to Westcott and Hort, it should be 'God our Father,' the pronoun 'our' being connected with 'Father' and not with 'Lord.' But the common reading has more support in the uncial manuscripts and the early versions than the reading adopted by Westcott and Hort. It should therefore be preferred. **And** (*from*) **our Lord Jesus Christ.** Here 'grace and peace' are supposed to come from Christ as well as from the Father.

The preposition 'from' is connected with both names, and marks them equally as sources of grace and peace; not one as the source and the other as the medium, but both as the source; a form of expression consistent with the doctrine of the Trinity, but inconsistent with any other view of Christ's relation to the Father. Paul conceived of divine grace as coming from Christ as well as the Father.

4. Who gave himself for our sins—that is, delivered himself up to death with reference to our sins, or on account of our sins—that is, to make expiation for them. See 3 : 12, seq., and Rom. 3 : 23, seq. This submission to death for the expiation of 'our sins' was in order to something further which is named in the next clause.

That he might deliver us from (*out of*) **this present evil world** (*age*). 'The present age' is here described as morally evil, because the men who give character to it are wicked. Compare with this language the words of Paul in the last part of the first chapter to the Romans. There can be no doubt of the awful moral condition of mankind in all parts of the known world when the apostle wrote this Epistle. Of course, deliverance out of the present evil age must mean deliverance out of its influence and its doom, a deliverance which could only be effected by rescuing men from the power and the penalty of sin. **According to the will of God and** (*even*) **our Father.** This expression is to be connected with the words 'gave himself for our sins,' as modified by the end sought, 'that he might deliver us,' etc. The voluntary death of Christ which was prerequisite to the salvation of men, is here declared to have been in accord with the will of God, who is at the same time characterized as 'our Father.' The pronoun 'our' naturally refers to Paul and his readers, regarded as Christians, and therefore to all who are the children of God by adoption. See Rom. 8:15-17. It cannot be safely interpreted as representing mankind, irrespective of union with Christ. The Greek original

5 To whom *be* glory for ever and ever. Amen.
6 I marvel that ye are so soon removed from him that called you into the grace of Christ unto another gospel:

5 and Father: to whom *be* the glory [1] for ever and ever. Amen.
6 I marvel that ye are so quickly removing from him who called you in the grace of Christ unto a

[1] Gr. *unto the ages of the ages.*

may, however, be translated 'according to the will of our God and Father'; and this translation is preferred by Lightfoot, on the ground that "the article not being necessary before God (θεοῦ), seems to be added to bind the two clauses together and connect both with 'our' (ἡμῶν)"—literally, 'of us.' But a comparison of the same expression in Phil. 4: 20; 1 Thess.1: 3; 3: 11, 13, with a somewhat similar expression in Rom. 1: 7; 1 Cor. 1: 3; 2 Cor. 1: 2, is favorable to the translation first given.

5. To whom be (*the***) glory forever and ever. Amen.** It is better to retain the article of the original text before the word 'glory,' for the glory referred to must be, either that which is due to God for his gracious will in the work of redemption (see the previous clause), or that which "especially and alone belongs to God" (Ellicott), and is therefore a definite glory.

Thus the apostle enriches his address and salutation to the churches of Galatia with the principal truths which he is about to defend as the only gospel. Among these truths are the sacrificial death of Christ, his resurrection by the power of God, his divinity and union with the Father, his direct agency in making Paul an apostle, and the fact that all this was done in obedience to the Father's will.

6–10. PAUL'S SURPRISE AT THE SUDDEN FALLING AWAY OF HIS READERS TO ANOTHER KIND OF GOSPEL, AND HIS DENUNCIATION OF THOSE WHO TAUGHT IT—A DENUNCIATION WHICH IS NATURAL BECAUSE HE DOES NOT SEEK HUMAN FAVOR BUT THE APPROVAL OF GOD.—Paul " expresses his astonishment at the sudden defection of the Galatians from the truth, characterizes the error which they had embraced, or were in danger of embracing, as an utter and fatal perversion of the gospel, and pronounces the conduct of those who had perplexed and misled them to be deserving of the severest reprobation and punishment. He takes the ground that the plan of salvation as preached by himself was the true and unalterable way of salvation, and that any different system, though taught by an angel from heaven, must be rejected at once as false, merely on the ground of such difference." (Hackett).

6. I marvel that ye are so soon removed (*so quickly removing*) **from him that called you into** (*in*) **the grace of Christ unto another gospel.** Dr. Hackett translates thus: "I marvel that ye are so soon removing from him who called you in the grace of Christ unto a different gospel." The abruptness with which Paul introduces the occasion for his Epistle reveals his intense and painful anxiety —an anxiety mingled with surprise and pressing for expression. The word translated ' marvel' occurs very often in the New Testament, and in the Common Version is frequently rendered ' wonder.' It may denote either a joyful or a painful surprise (Matt. 8: 10; Mark 6:6), a sudden and powerful emotion occasioned by something that is very admirable or very dreadful, and in either case unexpected. Whether the Greek words translated ' so quickly' have any reference to the short time which had passed since their conversion, or since the apostle's last visit to them, is doubtful. They may refer to the quickness with which the Galatians had yielded in some measure to the new doctrine, to the celerity or rapidity with which they were turning a friendly ear to the Judaizing teachers who had come among them. And if so, they furnish no clue to the date of the Epistle. At most, they point to the shortness of the time since the false teachers had begun their evil work in Galatia. See Introduction, V. According to the teaching of Paul elsewhere, the words 'him that called you' must refer to God the Father (Rom. 8: 30), though the call may have been ministered to them by the Holy Spirit and the word of truth. (2 Thess. 2: 14; Eph. 3: 6.) The words ' in the grace of Jesus Christ' are added to show that this divine calling has its ground or source in Christ. As Christians " were chosen in him before the foundation of the world" (Eph. 1: 4), so likewise are they called in his grace. The whole work of salvation springs from him. Hence, according to the Lord himself, prayer is to be offered in his name, and the answer to it from God will come

7 Which is not another; but there be some that trouble you, and would pervert the gospel of Christ.

8 But though we, or an angel from heaven, preach any other gospel unto you than that which we have preached unto you, let him be accursed.

9 As we said before, so say I now again, If any *man* preach any other gospel unto you than that ye have received, let him be accursed.

7 different gospel; ¹ which is not another *gospel*: only there are some that trouble you, and would pervert 8 the gospel of Christ. But though we, or an angel from heaven, should preach ²unto you any gospel ³other than that which we preached unto you, let 9 him be anathema. As we have said before, so say I now again, If any man preacheth unto you any gospel other than that which ye received, let him be

1 Or, *which is nothing else save that, etc*......2 Some ancient authorities omit *unto you*......3 Or, *contrary to that.*

---

in his name. (John 16: 23.) Paul is never weary of extolling the grace of Jesus Christ. And by the grace of Jesus Christ he evidently means the unmerited favor bestowed on men by reason of the voluntary death of Christ in their behalf, since he died a just One for unjust. See 1 Peter 3: 18. The expression 'another gospel' signifies in the original, 'another sort of gospel' or a gospel differing in kind from that which Paul had preached. The adjective here rendered 'another' (ἕτερον) is familiar to us in the first syllable of the English word heterogeneous, and is distinct from the word translated 'another' in the next clause.¹ Paul means by it a 'different' gospel.

7. Which is not another—that is, not another real gospel deserving the name and worthy to be called a second gospel. This it is not, because, though proclaimed as such, it is no gospel at all. **But there be some that trouble you, and would pervert the gospel of Christ.** Perhaps it would be wiser to translate the words rendered 'but,' (εἰ μή) 'save that' (Ellicott), for such is their ordinary meaning, and to explain the clause as follows: 'Which is *not* another, except in this sense that there are some that harass your minds and wish to pervert the gospel of Christ'; 'there are some who are troubling you by their desire and attempt to pervert the gospel.' The thought may also be expressed as follows, 'which is not another,' except that it is a peace-destroying perversion of the gospel; and so, a different kind of gospel. In other words, there are those among you whose teaching is no true gospel; but, though dealing with the gospel, and perhaps claiming to improve it, is a complete perver-

sion of it. "The Judaists bring you another gospel, but it is no gospel at all." (Ellicott.) 'The gospel of Christ' may here signify either the gospel proclaimed by him or the gospel concerning him—that is to say, good news issuing from him as its source, or good news concerning him as its object. The latter interpretation is preferable, though certainty cannot be gained.

8. But though (*even if*) **we, or an angel from heaven, preach any other gospel unto you than that which we have preached unto you, let him be accursed** —"But even if we, or an angel from heaven, should preach to you any other gospel contrary to that which we preached." (Hackett.) The Greek expression (παρ' ὅ) may mean 'contrary to that which,' or 'different from that which.' (Acts 18: 13; Rom. 1: 26; 1 Cor. 3: 11.) The first and sharper meaning is preferable here. The expression, 'which we preached (as good news) to you,' must refer to the preaching of Paul and his companions in Galatia, at his first and second visits to that province, the gospel which led to their conversion, and which, until recently, they had cherished as the power of God unto salvation without the help of Judaism. Thus Paul invokes the judgment of God upon any and every one who might pervert the gospel; and from the tremendous earnestness of his language it is necessary to believe that he had absolute confidence in the correctness of his own doctrine. He knew that what he preached was the very truth, as it is in Jesus; and he felt that the preaching of a different gospel would imperil the salvation of men and obscure the grace of God.

9. As we (*have*) **said before, so say I**

---

¹ Yet it is not always used in its distinctive sense, Often it appears to be simply equivalent to ἄλλος. Lightfoot says that ἄλλος is another as 'one besides,' ἕτερος another as 'one of two' .... Thus ἄλλος adds, while ἕτερος distinguishes. Now when our attention is confined to two objects, we naturally compare and contrast them: hence ἕτερος gets to signify 'unlike, opposite,' as Xenophon's "Cyropedia," VIII. 3, 8; Ex.

1: 8. "Thus while ἄλλος is generally confined to a negation of indentity, ἕτερος sometimes implies the negation of resemblance." See 2 Cor. 11: 4, where the two words are used appropriately, as they are here. In many cases, however, they will be interchangeable: compare Matt. 11: 3 with Luke 7: 20. Hesychius explains ἕτερον. ἄλλον· ἢ ἀλλοῖον· ἢ ἐν τοῖν δυοῖν· ἢ ἀριστερὸν, νέον δεύτερον.

10 For do I now persuade men, or God? or do I seek to please men? for if I yet pleased men, I should not be the servant of Christ.

11 But I certify you, brethren, that the gospel which was preached of me is not after man.

10 anathema. For am I now seeking the favour of men or of God? or am I striving to please men? if I were still pleasing men, I should not be a [1] servant of Christ.

11 For I make known to you, brethren, as touching the gospel which was preached by me, that it is not

---

[1] Gr. *bondservant.*

---

now again, if any man (one) preach any other gospel unto you than that ye have received, let him be accursed. See Revised Version.[1] The apostle doubtless refers in the first clause of this verse not to the preceding verse, but to his preaching, together with others, to the Galatians, when he visited them the second time; and, if so, he must then have detected (or foreseen) the presence of false teachers among them. For the imprecation is too strong to have been uttered when there were no signs of peril. From his language in this verse it is also manifest that Paul did not entertain the view which is now somewhat popular—that it is of little consequence what a man believes, provided his conduct is blameless. He knew that spiritual life must be nourished by truth, and not by error; and he was profoundly disturbed by the danger to which the Galatians were exposed.

But the apostle was aware that such language would seem to his readers severe and repulsive; therefore he explained his motive for using it.

10. For do I now persuade men, or God? The word 'persuade' ('am I now persuading') is here used in the sense of conciliating; and the apostle meant to affirm by this question that he was writing thus sternly with a view to the friendship of God, rather than the good will of men. In other words, he was not attempting to gain human favor, but divine. And by the next question—**Or do I seek (am I seeking) to please men?**—he denies with emphasis such a motive for his language, and then adds: **If I yet pleased (or, were still pleasing) men, I should not be the servant of Christ**—literally, Christ's bondservant. 'Yet,' or, *still*; that is, after all his experience. "The Greek for 'yet' (ἔτι) does not imply that Paul had ever been a timeserver." (Lightfoot.) No; but may it not imply that he had often sought to conciliate

men, though it was no time for him to do this now? 'Now' (ἄρτι) he could not be a bondservant of Christ, if he were to speak smooth things to the Galatians, or to hesitate to denounce those who were leading them to accept a different gospel, even one that weakened their faith in Christ. Others suppose that he may refer implicitly to what he had done before his conversion. (Hackett.) But this is less probable.

11, 12-2: 14. The Apostle Confirms his Teaching by Showing that he had not Received his Gospel from Men, but from Jesus Christ Himself, by Direct Revelation.—His theme is stated in verses 11 and 12, and its proof is given in the remainder of this chapter and the first fourteen verses of the next. Says Dr. Hackett: "He claims that his knowledge of the gospel is proved to be not of human, but of divine origin, negatively, by the fact that immediately on his conversion he entered on the full exercise of his office as an apostle, without any consultation with human advisers (1:16,17); that he preached the gospel for years without any intercourse, or even personal acquaintance, with the apostles; and that when at length he went to Jerusalem and saw some of their number, it was a visit of friendship merely, and had no relation whatever to his attainment of a more perfect knowledge of the Christian doctrines. (1:18-24.)"

Slightly different is the paraphrase of Lightfoot: "The revelation of his Son in me, the call to preach to the Gentiles, were acts of his good pleasure. Thus converted, I took no counsel of human advisers. I did not betake myself to the elder apostles, as I might naturally have done. I secluded myself in Arabia; and, when I emerged from my retirement, instead of going to Jerusalem I returned to Damascus."

11-12. Theme. But I certify to you, brethren. The Revised Version is better: *For*

---

[1] " As we have said before ... if any one preaches to you any other gospel contrary to that which ye received." (Hackett.)

12 For I neither received it of man, neither was I taught *it*, but by the revelation of Jesus Christ.

12 after man. For neither did I receive it from [1] man, nor was I taught it, but *it came to me* through reve-

I make known to you, brethren. Documentary evidence in favor of 'for' (γάρ) slightly out-weighs that in favor of 'but' (δέ), and may therefore be followed. The connection of thought is accordingly this: 'If I should seek to please men when the gospel is being per-verted as now, I should not be Christ's faithful bondservant, for this gospel was received by me from Christ himself and so expresses his will.' The formula 'I make known to you' shows that Paul attaches grave importance to what he is about to say. Compare 1 Cor. 12 : 3; 15 : 1; 2 Cor. 8 : 1, and the similar phrase, "I would not have you ignorant," in Rom. 1 : 13; 1 Cor. 10 : 1; 12 : 1; 2 Cor. 1 : 8; 1 Thess. 4 : 13. Observe, however, that he now addresses the members of the churches of Gal-atia as 'brethren.' They are not, then, in his estimation, apostates from Christ. They have not rejected the gospel of the grace of God. But they are in danger of doing this, for they are looking in the wrong direction, giving ear to dangerous error, and involved in a move-ment which, if continued, will separate them from God. And the whole object of his Epis-tle is to arrest this movement and bring them back to steadfast confidence in Christ as their sole and sufficient Saviour. So he addresses them heartily as 'brethren.' **That the gospel which was preached of me.** Com-pare Revised Version, *As touching the gospel which was preached by me.* Perhaps the full force of the original would be given by such a rendering as this: "in respect to the gospel which was preached as good news by me"— (τὸ εὐαγγέλιον τὸ εὐαγγελισθέν.) **Is not after man,** or, *that it is not after man.* That is, it is not of such a nature as it would have been if originated by man, it is not "after any human fashion or standard," it is neither in essence or object such a gospel as accords with human ideas of religion. Evidently Paul did not suppose that his gospel was a fruit of human speculation, or experience, or consciousness. Moral and religious evolution had no place in his conception of the origin of Christianity. He knew of man-made religions, and esteemed them wholly unlike the gospel—or the gospel wholly different from them.

12. For I neither received it of man, neither was I taught it. The 'I' is some-what emphatic, perhaps because there is an unexpressed reference to the older apostles; 'for neither did I, any more than the other apostles, receive it from (a) man, for example, Peter.' Sieffert objects to this as improbable, because there has been no allusion thus far to the other apostles, and suggests that the im-plied reference may be to the readers of the Epistle: 'I did not (as did you) receive it from a man.' But according to Buttmann the pronoun is sometimes inserted without being emphatic; and, if that be the case here, there is no tacit reference in it to any unnamed party. 'Neither (nor) was I taught it.' Lightfoot remarks that this clause was added to explain and enforce the foregoing state-ment, and thus to bring out the contrast with 'by revelation': "I received it, not by *in-struction* from man, but by *revelation* from Christ." But Ellicott holds that the verb 'was taught' points more to *subjective* appro-priation, and 'received' to *objective.* And Sieffert finds the distinction to be simply this, that one verb defines the mode of communi-cation while the other does not. Certainly the second verb is more definite as to manner than the first, and so gives natural progress to the course of thought. **But** (it came) **by** (*through*) **the revelation of Jesus Christ.** Omit the definite article before *revelation* as in the Revised Version, and understand that 'of Jesus Christ' means 'proceeding from Jesus Christ.' The Greek word translated 'revela-tion' signifies, literally, an uncovering, un-veiling, disclosing. But in the New Testa-ment it always denotes a disclosure of reli-gious truth before unknown. This disclosure is made to the soul either by God himself or by the ascended Christ, especially through the operation of the Holy Spirit (1 Cor. 2 : 10), and is thus distinguished from other modes of in-struction. (Thayer, *sub voce.*) It may be effected in part by a theophany or Christo-phany, but no visible manifestation is neces-sary to it. A partial revelation of Christian truth, before unknown, was made to Paul when Jesus appeared to him on the way to

13 For ye have heard of my conversation in time past in the Jews' religion, how that beyond measure I persecuted the church of God, and wasted it:

14 And profited in the Jews' religion above many my equals in mine own nation, being more exceedingly zealous of the traditions of my fathers.

13 lation of Jesus Christ. For ye have heard of my manner of life in time past in the Jews' religion, how that beyond measure I persecuted the church of God, and made havock of it: and I advanced in the Jews' religion beyond many of mine own age ¹among my countrymen, being more exceedingly zealous

1 Gr. in my race.

Damascus; but we cannot suppose that his knowledge of the gospel was completed at once. Says Ellicott: "It is a subject of continual discussion whether the teaching of St. Paul was the result of one single illumination, or of progressive development. . . . The most natural opinion would certainly seem to be this: that as, on the one hand, we may reverently presume that all the fundamental truths of the gospel would be fully revealed to St. Paul before he commenced preaching, so, on the other hand, it might have been ordained, that (in accordance with the laws of our spiritual nature) its deepest mysteries and profoundest harmonies should be seen and felt through the practical experiences of his apostolical labors." One cannot avoid conjecturing that during the first three years of his conversion a great part of the truth which he was to preach as the only gospel was revealed to him with divine clearness and evidence.

13-2 : 14. PROOF THAT HE DID NOT RECEIVE THE GOSPEL FROM MAN.

13. For ye have heard of my conversation in time past, etc. Compare Revised Version above. Probably from his own lips when he preached the gospel to them. "The history of his past career as a persecutor formed part of his preaching. See Acts 22: 2-21; 26 : 4-23; 1 Cor. 15 : 8-10." (Lightfoot.) So remarkable had been his spiritual life that a sketch of it would in many cases be not only appropriate, but almost necessary. **In the Jews' religion**—literally, *in Judaism*—means while he still observed the Jewish rites, and trusted in obedience to the Mosaic law for salvation. *In the Jewish religion* is perhaps the best translation. **How that beyond measure I persecuted the church of God, and wasted** (or, *made havoc of*) **it.** 'The church' may here signify, it is said, the Christian brotherhood, wherever they might be; but it may signify as well the first organized society of Christians, located at Jerusalem. To be sure, these were scattered abroad by the persecution that broke out after the stoning of

Stephen (Acts 9 : 1), and some of them doubtless went as far as Damascus, preaching the word there, and probably making disciples; but as yet there was but one church. By calling it 'the church *of God*,' Paul shows how sacred an institution he now felt it to be, and how deep was his compunction for attempting to lay it waste. Not that he speaks of his effort as a wholly futile attempt; he means rather to say that he was engaged for a time in persecuting and devastating it. This is the most obvious explanation of the tense of the Greek verbs. Many were put to death; many were imprisoned. (Acts 8 : 3; 9 : 1, 2; 26 : 10; 1 Cor. 15 : 9.) And the apostle mentions this to prove that he could not have received the gospel from men before his conversion, since he was at that time a fierce persecutor of the church.

14. And (that I) profited (advanced) in the Jews' religion above many, my equals in my own nation. "And went forward in Judaism beyond many companions of the same age." (Hackett.) 'My equals' means 'of my own age.' He outstripped the Jewish young men of his years in knowledge of the law, and in zeal for its observance. Writing to the Philippians concerning this part of his life, he describes himself as one who was, "as touching the law, a Pharisee; as touching zeal, persecuting the church; as touching the righteousness which is in the law, blameless." (3 : 5, 6.) Paul must then have been a very scrupulous as well as zealous Pharisee, a pronounced ritualist, and a conspicuous adversary of the new sect that was rising in Jerusalem. **Being more exceedingly zealous of (for) the traditions of my fathers.** This clause points out the sphere in which he excelled many of his own age. The adverb (περισσοτέρως) retains its comparative sense, 'more exceedingly.' He was far more of a zealot than many of his coevals for the traditions handed down by the rabbins from the fathers; he followed them, upheld them, asserted them with almost fanatical earnestness. Compare Matt. 5 : 21; 15 : 2; Mark 7 : 3. They were prob-

15 But when it pleased God, who separated me from my mother's womb, and called *me* by his grace,

16 To reveal his Son in me, that I might preach him among the heathen; immediately I conferred not with flesh and blood:

15 for the traditions of my fathers. But when it was the good pleasure of God, who separated me, *even from my mother's womb*, and called me through

16 his grace, to reveal his Son in me, that I might preach him among the Gentiles; immediately I

---

ably as sacred to him as the law of Moses; to some they appear to have been more sacred. So then it was certain that he had not been taught the Christian religion by any man before his conversion, and he now proceeds to show that he could not have been taught it in that way after his conversion. Says Lightfoot: "Then came my conversion. It was the work of God's grace. It was foreordained before I had any separate existence. It was not therefore due to any merits of my own; it did not spring from any principles of my own. The revelation of his Son in me, the call to preach to the Gentiles, were acts of his good pleasure. Thus converted, I took no counsel of human advisers. I did not betake myself to the elder apostles, as I might naturally have done. I secluded myself in Arabia, and when I emerged from my retirement, instead of going to Jerusalem, I returned to Damascus."

15, 16. But when it pleased God, who separated me, etc. The meaning of the original would be more exactly represented by the following translation: *But when he that set me apart from my mother's womb, and called me through his grace, was pleased to reveal his Son in me, that I might preach him among the Gentiles,* etc. 'Set me apart' —that is, assigned or devoted me to a special work, even the preaching of Christ to the Gentiles. Compare Rom. 1 : 1 and Acts 13 : 2. The word 'separated' in the Common and the Revised Versions is ambiguous. Paul represents himself as singled out and set apart by the will of God from his very birth to the apostleship. And the next clause, 'called me by his grace,' directs attention to another act of God—namely, the divine agency in his conversion. The same verb is used in Rom. 8 : 30: "And whom he foreordained, them he also called." This divine calling comprehends all that God does to awaken the moral nature of a sinner and bring him to repentance. In Paul's case it was the supernatural effulgence and the voice of Christ, together with the work of the Holy Spirit in his soul, which had so powerful an effect on his moral

nature, and led him so quickly into the new life. The change of that moment was radical, permanent, and wholly of grace. "Observe," says Lightfoot, "how words are accumulated to tell upon the one point on which he is insisting—the sole agency of God as distinct from his own efforts." 'To reveal his Son in me'—that is, within me, in my spirit or consciousness, so that I for the first time perceived his true character and work. This prepares one for the next clause far better than does the explanation 'through me,' which is favored by Lightfoot and others, appealing to ver. 24 and 1 Tim. 1 : 16. Besides, there is great weight in Ellicott's view, that wherever the primary meaning [of the preposition *ἐν*] gives a sense which cannot be objected to dogmatically or exegetically, we are bound to abide by it. Both *subjectively*, by deep inward revelations, as well as *objectively*, by outward manifestations, was the great apostle prepared for the work of the ministry."

That I might preach him among the heathen (or, *Gentiles*). It was God's good pleasure to reveal his Son in the heart of Paul, in order that Paul might preach him among the Gentiles. Are we then authorized by this language to say that one of the reasons why God's grace was imparted to Paul was the extraordinary service, which, when converted, he would be qualified and employed to render in preaching to the Gentiles? It is an interesting and far-reaching question which we thus propose to the reader, without giving a categorical answer to it ourselves. **Immediately I conferred not with flesh and blood.** The adverb 'immediately,' or, *straightway* appears to modify, not only this statement, but also the two following statements. He first declares what he did not do, and then what he did do, directly after his conversion. Of course, the adverb is not to be so urged as to make it contradict the account of Luke, that Paul abode three days in Damascus before his sight was restored. Its use in other parts of the New Testament forbids so narrow an interpretation. See 3 John 14. Like many other words, it is more or less affected by

17 Neither went I up to Jerusalem to them which were apostles before me; but I went into Arabia, and returned again unto Damascus.
18 Then after three years I went up to Jerusalem to see Peter, and abode with him fifteen days.

17 conferred not with flesh and blood: neither went I up to Jerusalem to them who were apostles before me: but I went away into Arabia; and again I returned unto Damascus.
18 Then after three years I went up to Jerusalem [1] to visit Cephas, and tarried with him fifteen days.

1 Or, *become acquainted with.*

the context.[1] For the meaning of 'flesh and blood' compare Matt. 16: 17: "Flesh and blood did not reveal it unto thee." The phrase appears to be equivalent to weak human nature, viewed probably in contrast with the divine source from which Paul had received his gospel.

17. Neither went I up to Jerusalem to them which were apostles before me. There is some uncertainty about the text in this clause. The Revised Version, Westcott and Hort, and Tischendorf, Eighth Edition, have 'went up' (ἀνῆλθον) while Ellicott says that this reading "seems obviously a correction, and is rejected by all the best editors." (1859.) But he would not write thus at the present time.[2] By 'those who were apostles before me' Paul means the Twelve, or as many of them as were then at Jerusalem. As to James, the Lord's brother, nothing need be said at this point. His position will be noticed in explaining ver. 19. **But I went** (*away*) **into Arabia.** It has been commonly supposed that Paul went into some part of Arabia not far from Damascus. But this is by no means certain, and the opinion that he visited the region about Sinai is strenuously defended by Lightfoot and others. See his general note on "St. Paul's sojourn in Arabia." Whether he went into Arabia for the purpose of preaching the gospel, or for the purpose of preparing himself to do this work more effectually, after a period of solitary communion with God, no one can say. In either case he was doubtless guided by the Spirit of Christ to do as he did; and in either

case he was unable during this period to receive instruction from men. As to the length of time passed in Arabia nothing is said. It could not have been more than three years (see ver. 18), and probably was not less than two. Compare the account in Acts 9 : 20-23. In his brief sketch of Paul's life, Luke had no occasion to speak of this sojourn in Arabia. **And returned again unto Damascus.** The little word 'again' connects his conversion with Damascus, though nothing is said of that city in the previous verses. But we know from the Acts that Paul was in that city during three days directly after Christ's appearing to him in the way, and the word 'again' here implies that he left Damascus to go into Arabia. The two records, therefore, complement and confirm each other, yet without affording the slightest evidence of any intention to do this.

18. Then, after three years, I went up to Jerusalem. The date from which he reckons the 'three years' must be the time of conversion, not the time of his return to Damascus. For the former was the great epoch of his life, while his return to Damascus was a comparatively unimportant event. Besides, it would be difficult to make out any reasonable chronology of the apostle's life if his first visit to Jerusalem took place six years after his conversion. With this view most interpreters agree—for example, Winer, Fritzsche, Rückert, Usteri, Olshausen, DeWette, Hilgenfeld, Ewald, Wieseler, Hofmann, Meyer, Sieffert, Ellicott, Lightfoot, Hackett, Conybeare and Howson, and others. This is the

---

[1] The compound Greek word translated 'conferred' is worthy of particular notice, though well explained in Thayer's Lexicon. προσ-ανα-τίθημι. 1. *To lay up in addition.* 2. Middle. (a) *To lay upon one's self in addition; to undertake besides.* (b) With a dative of the person *to put one's self upon another by going to him*—i. e., *to commit or betake one's self to another*, for the purpose of consulting him, hence *to consult, to take one into counsel* (Authorized Version, *to confer with*).

[2] In support of ἀνῆλθον Tischendorf (Eighth Ed.) appeals to ℵ A K L P with the Peschito and the Coptic,

the Armenian and the Ethiopic, while in support of ἀπῆλθον he appeals to B D E F G, the Syriac, etc. The documents for one are therefore nearly equal to those for the other, and the probabilities of change from one to the other by transcribers are indecisive. For a transcriber might unintentionally have written ἀνῆλθον instead of ἀπῆλθον because the former was so often used of going to Jerusalem, or he might have written ἀπῆλθον instead of ἀνῆλθον because his eye fell at the moment on the former verb in the next clause.

19 But other of the apostles saw I none, save James the Lord's brother.
20 Now the things which I write unto you, behold, before God, I lie not.
21 Afterwards I came into the regions of Syria and Cilicia:

19 But other of the apostles saw I none, [1] save James 20 the Lord's brother. Now touching the things which I write unto you, behold, before God, I 21 not. Then I came into the regions of Syria and

first journey of Paul to Jerusalem, narrated by Luke in Acts 9 : 26.

To see (or, visit) Peter. More exactly, to become acquainted with Cephas. Evidently, Cephas or Peter was a very prominent apostle in Jerusalem at that time. According to the Acts he was the principal figure among the apostles—bold, outspoken, enterprising, a natural leader of men, and so occupying the position which he was qualified to fill. Hence, although Paul was already established in the Christian faith and abundantly able to preach the gospel, it was perfectly natural for him to desire the acquaintance of Peter, and of any other apostles who might then be in the holy city. And abode (tarried) with him fifteen days. Too short a period for any very thorough study of Christian truth under the tuition of Peter. Paul considers this self-evident. The Galatians could not possibly believe that such knowledge as he possessed of the way of life through Christ had been gained in a fortnight from any human teacher. Besides, as we learn from the narrative of Luke, Paul was "going in and going out at Jerusalem," during those fifteen days, "preaching boldly in the name of the Lord: and he spake and disputed against the Grecian Jews; but they went about to kill him." (Acts 9 : 28.) Paul did not deem it necessary to say all this: it was enough to remind his readers of his purpose in going up to Jerusalem, and of the short time which he spent in that city.

19. But other of the apostles saw I none, save James the Lord's brother. The Seiffert-Meyer Commentary says: "Thus this James is distinguished from the circle of the Twelve, to which Peter belonged; but is,

nevertheless, numbered with the apostles in the wider sense. Compare 1 Cor. 15 : 5. This explains the supplementary mention of his name. 'James the Lord's brother' was not James, son of Alpheus, as many have supposed, but a natural brother of Jesus (Matt. 13 : 35; Mark 6 : 3), a son of Mary, James the Just (Hegesippus in Eusebius 2 : 23), from birth a Nazarite, who only believed after the resurrection of Jesus (1 Cor. 15 : 7; Acts 1 : 14), but obtained very high apostolic esteem among the Jewish Christians (2 : 9), and became the honored bishop of the church at Jerusalem." This view is upheld by a majority of modern scholars; for example, by Olshausen, De Wette, Hilgenfeld, Wieseler, Lightfoot, Meyer and Sieffert.[1]

20. Now the things which I write unto you, behold, before God, I lie not. A solemn asseveration of the truth of what he has just written as to the purpose and result of his visit to Jerusalem, as far as they had any bearing upon the source of his knowledge of the gospel. He evidently makes this solemn appeal to God for the truth of his words, because his readers could have no other evidence as to the time which he then spent in Jerusalem, or as to the purpose which led him to go there. It looks as if he was aware that the Judaizers in Galatia had represented him as having received the gospel, at second hand, from Peter and other apostles, and that it was desirable for him to show the utter falsity of their representation. The Greek construction may be represented by the following version: "Now as to what I am writing to you, before God I declare that I lie not." (Ellicott.) Compare 2 Tim. 2 : 14; 4 : 1.

21. Afterwards I came into the regions

[1] "Are we to translate 'I saw no other apostle save James,' or, 'I saw no other apostle, but only James'? It will be seen that the question is not whether εἰ μὴ ('save'), retains its exceptive force or not, for this it seems always to do, but whether the exception refers to the whole clause or to the verb alone. That the latter is quite a possible construction will appear from Matt. 12 : 4; Luke 4 : 26, 27; Gal. 2 : 16; Rev. 21 : 27. But, on the other hand, the sense of ἕτερον ('other') naturally links it with εἰ μὴ ('save'), from which it cannot be separated without harshness, and ἕτερον ('other') carries τῶν ἀποστόλων ('the apostles') with it. It seems, then, that James is here called an apostle, though it does not, therefore, follow that he was one of the twelve." (Lightfoot.) See Thayer's "Lexicon," under εἰ μὴ, III, c. 8, β.

22 And was unknown by face unto the churches of Judea which were in Christ:
23 But they had heard only, That he which persecuted us in times past now preacheth the faith which once he destroyed.
24 And they glorified God in me.

22 Cilicia. And I was still unknown by face unto the churches of Judea which were in Christ; but they only heard say, He that once persecuted us now preacheth the faith of which he once made havock; 24 and they glorified God in me.

of Syria and Cilicia. According to Acts 9 : 30, Paul appears to have sailed from Cesarea to Tarsus in Cilicia, from which place he passed into Syria, preaching in the two provinces four or five years. See Hackett on Acts 9 : 30. His object in this passage is simply to direct attention to the regions where he preached as *remote* from Jerusalem, where the apostles then were ; and he therefore mentions the provinces in the order of their importance. "Cilicia," says Ewald, "was constantly little better than an appendage of Syria." "It is also to be noticed that these two countries are always named in that order (see Acts 15 : 23, 41), and that order agrees with the land route from Jerusalem to Cilicia, which was the one more commonly taken. Hence, Paul may have adhered to that order in Gal. 1 : 21 from the force of association, though in this instance he went first to Cilicia, and from there made missionary excursions into Syria." (Hackett on Acts 9 : 30.) It should be added that Paul may have preached at this time more extensively in Syria than in Cilicia, and that in recalling this period of his ministry, the former province, on that account, took precedence in his mind of the latter. Thus there is no reason to suppose any contradiction between this passage and the account given by Luke. The difference between the two rather establishes our confidence in both, when properly interpreted, for it demonstrates their independence.

22. And was unknown by face unto the churches of Judea which were in Christ. By 'the churches of Judea' must be meant the churches of the province, outside of Jerusalem. For the apostle has before spoken of his brief sojourn in that city, and Luke describes, in a few powerful words, his public efforts there. Many of the churches in Jerusalem had, therefore, seen his face and heard his voice. But this was not the case with the churches of the province generally. ' By face,' or, in respect to face—that is, per-

sonal appearance, though he was known to them by report, as the next verse clearly states, and as might be safely inferred from the nature of the case. Note the plural— there were *churches* of Judea.

23. But they had heard only—or, *But they were only hearing.* This was a report which, during those years of the apostle's life of which so little is recorded, they were hearing again and again. **He which (*that*) persecuted us in times past—that is, 'was our persecutor, known as such, distinguished as such beyond others.' Now preacheth the faith which once he destroyed.** To 'preach faith' may be to preach the duty or importance or nature of subjective faith in Christ; but to 'preach *the* faith' is to preach the gospel, regarded as a message of which faith in Christ is the central and distinctive truth. Hackett explains the expression in Acts 6 : 7 as meaning "the faith-system—that is, the gospel"; and Lightfoot remarks, "It is a striking proof of the large space occupied by 'faith' in the mind of the infant church, that it should so soon have passed into a synonym of the gospel. See Acts 6 : 7." Compare, also, Jude 3. This appears to be the more obvious and correct view, though many deny that the word faith is used in the New Testament of anything but the subjective act. Certainly Paul preached the doctrine of faith in Christ; and it was those who received this doctrine and believed in Christ whom he persecuted and wasted. So 'the faith' here represents, first, the gospel, and, secondly, those who received it. The core, the heart of both, was faith in the Lord Jesus Christ.

24. And they glorified God in me—that is, they found in me occasion to praise God. "He does not say that they marveled at me, they praised me, they were struck with admiration, but he attributes all to grace. 'They glorified God,' he says, 'in me.'" (Chrysostom.)

CHAPTER II.

THEN fourteen years after I went up again to Jeru- | 1 Then after the space of fourteen years I went
salem with Barnabas, and took Titus with me also. | up again to Jerusalem with Barnabas, taking Titus

Ch. 2: "Again, he claims that the same thing—[that his knowledge of the gospel is not of human but of divine origin]—is proved affirmatively by the fact that, on his coming at a later period into fuller connection with the apostles, his views of truth were sanctioned by them, as perfectly coincident with their own, though they had been taught personally by our Lord (2:1-6); that he was recognized by them as standing in all respects, officially, on a level with themselves (2:7-10); and that, so far from having acted at any time in subordination to them, or having acknowledged any dependence on them, he had in one instance opposed his own authority to that of one of the most eminent among them. (2:11-13.) In the controversy at Antioch, he had not shrunk from reproving Peter himself publicly and to his face for having practically abandoned the great principle of justification by faith alone, inasmuch as he had timidly concealed for a time his real convictions, and acted as if Jewish rites must be superadded to faith in Christ as essential to salvation. (2:14-21.)" (Hackett.)

1-10. PAUL'S GOSPEL AND APOSTLESHIP RECOGNIZED BY JAMES, PETER, AND JOHN AT A CONVENTION IN JERUSALEM, WHEREIN THE DUTY OF BELIEVING GENTILES TOWARD THE JEWISH LAW WAS CONSIDERED.

1. Then fourteen years after (or, *after the space of fourteen years*[1]) **I went up again to Jerusalem with Barnabas,** etc. With which of the apostle's visits to Jerusalem, mentioned by Luke in the Acts, can this be identified? See Acts 9 : 26; 11 : 30; 15 : 1, seq.; 18 : 22; 21 : 15. Obviously with the third, if similarity of purpose is any guide to the truth. For this is the only one of the five, except the last, which Luke describes as having to do with questions allied to those mentioned by Paul in the first part of this chapter, and this Epistle was certainly written before his last visit to Jerusalem. His first and last visits may therefore be left out of the question, and our inquiry restricted to the second, third, and fourth. All that Luke says of the second

visit is comprised in two verses: "And the disciples [at Antioch], every man according to his ability, determined to send relief unto the brethren that dwelt in Judea; which also they did, sending it to the elders by the hand of Barnabas and Paul." There is nothing in this which suggests, even remotely, such transactions as the apostle describes in the passage before us. Still more briefly does Luke notice the fourth visit of Paul: "And when they had landed at Cesarea, he [Paul] went up and saluted the church [at Jerusalem], and went down to Antioch."

But it may be said that the account of Luke in the fifteenth chapter of the Acts differs very greatly from the account here given by Paul. This is true, yet the two accounts relate to the same general subject, and may without difficulty be seen to complement each other. Luke's account is that of a historian desiring to present a sketch of the proceedings in so far as they affected all the churches; Paul's account is that of a man who desires to establish a single point, namely, that his teaching and authority were admitted to be Christian and apostolic by the greatest of the Twelve. Studied in this light, the two accounts will be seen to belong together.

But from what event is the period of 'fourteen years' reckoned? Obviously, from his going up to Jerusalem to make the acquaintance of Peter, as previously described. (1:18.) This *terminus a quo* is suggested by the word 'again,' and must be accepted as the one in Paul's mind, unless there are insuperable objections to it. The weightiest objections are chronological, but they do not appear to be decisive. Says Lightfoot: "As the latter visit is calculated independently to have taken place A. D. 51, the date of the first visit will according to this view be thrown back to about A. D. 38, and that of the conversion to about A. D. 36, the Jewish mode of reckoning being adopted." This seems to us a more natural interpretation than to suppose that Paul meant fourteen years after his conversion. Compare Ellicott on the passage, with

[1] Compare Mark 2: 1; Acts 24: 17.

2 And I went up by revelation, and communicated unto them that gospel which I preach among the Gentiles, but privately to them which were of reputation, lest by any means I should run, or had run, in vain.

2 also with me. And I went up by revelation; and I laid before them the gospel which I preach among the Gentiles, but privately before them who [1] were of repute, lest by any means I should be running,

---

[1] Or, are.

Conybeare and Howson, chapter vii. 'With Barnabas' agrees with Luke's narrative in Acts 15 : 2, which represents Paul and Barnabas as sent by the church at Antioch to the apostles and elders at Jerusalem because of dissensions in respect to the necessity of circumcision to salvation. From that narrative it appears that "certain other" members of the church were sent in company with Paul and Barnabas.

And took Titus with me also. The form of expression here employed makes Paul himself the leading person in this company, for in some sense he took with him Barnabas and Titus *also*. The latter may have been included in Luke's "certain other" brethren, though Paul appears to have wished him to go, perhaps as a representative of heathen converts to the truth. For other notices of him, see 2 Cor. 2 : 13; 7 : 6, 13, seq.; 8 : 6, 16, 23; 12 : 18; 2 Tim. 4 : 10; Titus 1 : 4.

2. And I went up by revelation—that is, in accordance with 'revelation,' or, perhaps, with a revelation. This revelation may have preceded and occasioned the action of the church, or it may have followed that action, assuring Paul of his duty to go up to Jerusalem for the purpose contemplated. In either case it was natural for the historian Luke to relate the action of the brethren in respect to Paul's visit to Jerusalem, and equally natural for Paul to speak in this letter of the special revelation by which he was moved to do the same thing. **And communicated unto them that gospel which I preach among the Gentiles.** Paul made to 'them'—that is, to the Christians at Jerusalem—a careful statement of the gospel which he was preaching among the Gentiles. This was a wise proceeding, for he had reason to fear that it had been more or less misrepresented by his detractors. **But privately to them which (who) were of reputation.** This is not to be understood as explaining the previous clause, and denying that there was any public conference for the same purpose, but as calling attention to certain private meetings with the leaders of the church, by which their influence in favor

of Christian truth and freedom might be gained for the public conference. "The private consultation was a wise precaution to avoid misunderstanding: the public conference was a matter of necessity to obtain recognition of the freedom of the Gentile churches." (Lightfoot.) Compare Acts 15 : 4, 6, 12, 22. **Lest by any means I should run**—(literally *be running*), **or had run in vain**—that is, 'in vain' so far as concerned establishing the freedom of the Gentile Christians from the law of Moses, without a breach with the Jewish Christians. For however true and divine his doctrine might be, if it was not understood and accepted by such men as James, Peter, and John, who were pillars of the church at Jerusalem, his work in the present and in the past would be to a great extent neutralized. Says Pfleiderer: "We may imagine in what a painful situation the apostle . . . found himself. If the party zealous from the Law should be successful with their demand that the believing Gentiles must by circumcision submit to the Jewish Law, and if it should be confirmed that in this demand they really had the parent church, together with the apostles on their side, the mission to the Gentiles was at an end, and the life-work of the apostle to the heathen was hopeless. . . . If Paul had, on the other hand, simply ignored the demands of the Judaizers, without coming to any understanding with the earlier apostles and obtaining their sanction of his Gentile mission, with its freedom from the Law, he would have severed the connection of his heathen churches with the parent church, and the Gentile church, thus isolated from the very first and degraded to a sect, would hardly have been able long to maintain its existence. The continuance or the destruction of his life work depended therefore now, to Paul's mind, on whether he succeeded in obtaining from the parent church and its leaders the acknowledgment of their Christian fellowship for his Gentile Christians as such." ("The influence of the Apostle Paul on Christianity," p. 85.) The clause before us is a very difficult one to interpret. Ellicott gives

3 But neither Titus, who was with me, being a Greek, was compelled to be circumcised:
4 And that because of false brethren unawares brought in, who came in privily to spy out our liberty

3 or had run, in vain. But not even Titus who was with me, being a Greek, was compelled to be cir-
4 cumcised: [1] and that because of the false brethren privily brought in, who came in privily to spy out

1 Or, but it was because of.

the following version: "Lest by any means I might be running, or have run, in vain." The verb 'run' represents Paul's apostolic ministry under the figure of a race. His work was performed as eagerly, and strenuously as the running of an athlete in the race course, and at this time he was not without apprehension of losing the prize for which he had striven. Unless he could gain the support of James, Peter, and John, with most of the church at Jerusalem, there was no human prospect of maintaining the liberty of the Gentile churches, without breaking wholly with the converts from Judaism. Hence his private interviews with these men, as well as his public explanation of the gospel which he preached. The verb 'run' is here used first in the present subjunctive, and in the aorist indicative. Compare 1 Thess. 3 : 5. "In the second clause the change of mood from the subjunctive (τρέχω) to the indicative (ἔδραμον) is rendered necessary by the change of tense, since the consequences of the past were no longer contingent but inevitable." (Lightfoot.)

3. But neither (*not even*) **Titus, who was with me, being a Greek, was compelled to be circumcised.** The phrase 'being a Greek' is to be understood as concessive; 'who was with me, although he was a Greek,' and therefore of course uncircumcised. The language of this sentence, especially when taken with what follows, plainly implies that his circumcision was insisted upon so strongly that refusal was difficult. Nor is this surprising. For the question to be practically settled at this time was deemed of vital importance by the Judaistic party as well as by Paul and Barnabas. Titus, an uncircumcised Greek, was there associated with Paul, and nothing could seem more indispensable to the Judaistic spirit than his circumcision. To see him there as a Greek was like Haman's seeing Mordecai at the king's gate. On the other hand, it was impossible for Paul to consent to his circumcision, even for the sake of peace, for it would be surrendering in a crucial instance the very principle for which

he was contending; namely, that Gentile sinners could be saved through faith in Christ without submitting to the Mosaic law. There is no evidence in this passage, however, or in the narrative of Luke in the Acts, that any of the apostles sympathized with those who demanded the circumcision of Titus, though it is perhaps conceivable that they may have advised him to yield the point for the sake of peace. Yet we discover no hint of even this, and the later weakness of Peter must not be allowed to cast any shadow upon his action at Jerusalem. In the narrative of Luke he appears as the consistent advocate of admitting Gentiles to Christian fellowship upon their acceptance of Christ.

4. And that, because of the false brethren unawares (*privily*) **brought in.** This difficult verse is best explained by regarding it as a continuation of the preceding sentence, from which it should be separated by a comma only. Some interpreters hold that it was added in order to show why the pressure to have Titus circumcised was ineffectual. That pressure was occasioned by the presence of certain false brethren, who were more Jewish than Christian, and whose aim and spirit were thoroughly hostile to the principles which Paul was there to sustain. And Paul's language is thought to imply that he might have consented to the circumcision of Titus, if it had been called for by the scruples of 'the weaker brethren,' instead of the bigotry of *false* brethren. But is this at all probable? Can we suppose that, after what had occurred at Antioch (Acts 15 : 1. seq.), Paul would have consented to pacify weak consciences by the circumcision of Titus? Or that in this Epistle to the Galatians he would have intimated the possibility of such consent? The circumstances of his visit to Jerusalem and of his writing this letter alike forbid the thought. It seems better, therefore, to suppose that the apostle added these words to point out the occasion of this unsuccessful attempt to secure the circumcision of Gentiles—the occasion of this entire transaction, especially as it was illustrated in the case of Titus. Not even

which we have in Christ Jesus, that they might bring us into bondage:

our liberty which we have in Christ Jesus, that

Titus, who was present with me (to say nothing of others less conspicuous, or of the Gentiles in general), was compelled by the voice of the church to be circumcised, and that on account of the false brethren, etc. The whole controversy, he means to say, was occasioned by these brethren. It was a desire to satisfy them which led to the proposal to circumcise Titus. It was their character and aim which led Paul and Barnabas to withstand them in Antioch and later in Jerusalem. And it was precisely these, their spirit and aim, which weakened their influence in the church, and rendered it possible, humanly speaking, for the friends of Christian liberty to prevail.

The only other view which suits the connection is this, that the conjunction (δέ) should be translated 'but,' and the ellipsis be supplied as follows: 'but (this came to pass) on account of the false brethren surreptitiously introduced.' That is, the entire transaction, embracing the effort to have Titus circumcised, and the relinquishment of that effort as impracticable or wrong, was occasioned by the presence and influence of the false brethren, etc. It is difficult to decide between this and the preceding interpretation. Either of them is consistent with the language and the situation, but neither of them is obvious. The passage is confessedly obscure, and scholars have thus far labored in vain to reach a perfectly satisfactory interpretation of it.

"Three ideas," remarks Jowett, "seem to be struggling for expression in these ambiguous clauses [ver. 3–5]: (1) Titus was not circumcised; (2) though an attempt was made by the false brethren to compel him; (3) which as a matter of principle we thought it so much the more our duty to resist." "What part was taken in the discussion by the apostles of the circumcision? . . . On the whole it seems probable that they recommended St. Paul to yield the point, as a charitable concession to the prejudices of the Jewish converts;

but convinced at length by his representations that such a concession, at such a time, would be fatal, they withdrew their counsel, and gave him their support." (Lightfoot.) As previously remarked, this conjecture as to the first advice of the apostles has no proper foundation in the language of Paul or of Luke, and should not be received with any great confidence. The Greek word (παρεισάκτους) translated 'brought in privily' might be rendered 'insidiously brought in.' Possibly it has the active sense, 'who have stolen in.' The figure is that of spies, let in or stealing in. If the word is used here in the passive sense, there must have been Christians in the church at Jerusalem, and perhaps elsewhere, who facilitated the entrance of these false brethren, knowing more of their views and spirit than were openly avowed.

Who came in privily to spy out our liberty which we have in Christ Jesus, that they might bring us into bondage. They were Pharisees in disguise, coming into the church to bring it under the law of Moses, as interpreted by Rabbinic tradition, or, as Paul often calls it, the law of works. Their interest was in the law rather than in the gospel, and they crept into the church for the purpose of upholding ritualism and resisting the progress of spiritual freedom, for the purpose of bringing the Christians back to Judaism. This finishes the apostle's brief but vigorous characterization of the extreme Judaists whom he found in the church at Jerusalem, and we have no reason to pronounce it harsh or untrue in any particular.

Notice, on the other hand, his view of the Christian's state when united with Christ. It is one of liberty. His service of Christ springs from love and gratitude, not from fear. He is not under law, as a means of acceptance with God, but under grace. 'Freedom' is here freedom from obligation to obey the law of Moses as a means of salvation.[1]

---

[1] On the use of ἵνα with the future, Lightfoot says: "It is found several times in the New Testament with the future, and sometimes even with the indicative present, as in 4 : 17. This, though not a classical usage, is justified by similar constructions of ὅπως, ὄφρα in classical writers." Ellicott is more doubtful, saying: "Although this reading is confirmed by a decided preponderance of uncial authority [A B C D E (with ℵ)], and the improbability of a correction very great, still the instances of ἵνα with the future are so very few, and are not justified in saying more than this, that the future appears used to convey the idea of duration, or perhaps, rather, of issue, sequence, more distinctly than the more usual aorist subjunctive."

5 To whom we gave place by subjection, no, not for an hour; that the truth of the gospel might continue with you.

6 But of those who seemed to be somewhat, whatsoever they were, it maketh no matter to me; God accepteth no man's person: for they who seemed to be somewhat in conference added nothing to me:

5 they might bring us into bondage; to whom we gave place in the way of subjection, no, not for an hour; that the truth of the gospel might continue with you. But from those who [1] were reputed to be somewhat ([2] whatsoever they were, it maketh no matter to me: God accepteth not man's person — they, I say, who were of repute imparted nothing to

1 Or, are......2 Or, what they once were.

5. To whom we gave place by subjection, no, not for an hour. A more literal rendering would be: 'To whom we yielded not even for an hour by the subjection' demanded of us.[1] **That the truth of the gospel might continue with you.** The controlling motive in the minds of Paul and Barnabas was a desire to have the good news of salvation by grace, without the deeds of the Law, remain in their possession as a permanent blessing.

6. But of those who seemed to be somewhat—or, as in the Revised Version, *But from those who were reputed to be somewhat.* Here the sentence breaks off, the apostle turning aside from the thought which he has begun to express, to make, by way of parenthesis, the remarks of the next two clauses, and then resuming his opening thought in a different construction. If, then, we learn his first thought from the last clause of the verse, he began to say : 'But from those reputed to be somewhat nothing was communicated to me,' or 'added to my knowledge of the gospel.' Yet he turns away from this thought when it is but half expressed to remark concerning 'those reputed to be somewhat,' **whatsoever they were, it maketh no matter** (*difference*) **to me,** or, in other words, is a matter of no account to me. Yet another rendering of this clause is possible : " What they formerly were makes no difference with me." In this case the word translated 'formerly' (ποτέ) is an adverb of time, as it is said to be in every other passage of the New Testament where it occurs. If so understood here, Paul means to say that their former connection with Jesus as his disciples is really of no consequence to him, for God does not grant his favor on account of any outward advantage of one man over another. And if so understood, the words clearly imply that the assailants of Paul's apostolic authority extolled the

other apostles because they once enjoyed the personal teaching of Christ and depreciated Paul because he never had it. **God accepteth no man's** (Revised Version, *not man's*) **person.** The latter rendering is equivalent to saying : No outward differences between men affect God's treatment of them. He looks at them as they are and accepts them for what they are worth. Wordly distinctions count for nothing with him. The circumstance that James, Peter, and John were acquainted with Jesus and instructed by him, during his earthly life, gives them no advantage in the sight of God over one who had received the same knowledge of Christ by revelation. The expression 'to be somewhat' is not in itself depreciatory, though it may be made so by the context. Sieffert imagines that it here betrays "a certain irritation in respect to his adversaries who would not admit his equality with the original apostles, as if 'the being somewhat' belonged especially to them." And Lightfoot remarks that "the exact shade of meaning which it bears must always be determined by the context. Here it is depreciatory, not indeed of the Twelve themselves, but of the extravagant and exclusive claims set up for them by the Judaizers."

For they who seemed, etc. (or, as Revised Version, *They, I say, who were of repute imparted nothing to me*). The order of the Greek words makes the pronoun 'me' at the beginning of the phrase emphatic: 'to me, I say, they who were of repute imparted nothing'—that is, nothing which pertains to the gospel, no knowledge in respect to Christ or the way of life which I did not have before. Indeed, the verb probably signifies to make a communication to, and Paul denies that they communicated any religious truth to him. It seems, therefore, that his communications to them were so full and clear that they did not make any attempt to instruct him.

---

[1] Dr Hackett translates: "To whom we yielded the subjection (εἴξαμεν τῇ ὑποταγῇ), no, not for an hour,' and adds: "Our translators make the τῇ ὑποταγῇ almost a tautological repetition of εἴξαμεν. It is *the subjection* demanded in this matter of circumcision which is meant."

7 But contrariwise, when they saw that the gospel of the uncircumcision was committed unto me, as the gospel of the circumcision was unto Peter;
8 (For he that wrought effectually in Peter to the apostleship of the circumcision, the same was mighty in me toward the Gentiles;)
9 And when James, Cephas, and John, who seemed to be pillars, perceived the grace that was given unto me, they gave to me and Barnabas the right hands of fellowship; that we should go unto the heathen, and they unto the circumcision.

7 me: but contrariwise, when they saw that I had been intrusted with the gospel of the uncircumcision, even
8 as Peter with the gospel of the circumcision (for he who wrought for Peter unto the apostleship of the circumcision wrought for me also unto the Gentiles);
9 and when they perceived the grace that was given unto me, James and Cephas and John, they who 1 were reputed to be pillars, gave to me and Barnabas the right hands of fellowship, that we should go unto the Gentiles, and they unto the circumcision;

1 Or, are.

It is, perhaps, worthy of notice that the Greek expression here used (οἱ δοκοῦντες) may signify either 'they who were of repute' or 'they who are of repute.' Lightfoot greatly prefers the present tense, thinking that Paul has in mind the reputation enjoyed by them among the Jewish Christians at the time when he wrote this letter. For they were now lauded by the men who were aiming to pervert the gospel among the Galatians as well as honored by the church at Jerusalem. In either case, the meaning of the passage is pertinent and forcible, and with either translation it agrees with all that is known concerning the history of the early churches.[1]

7. But contrariwise, when they saw, etc., the remainder of the verse better, as in the Revised Version, *that I had been entrusted with the gospel of the uncircumcision even as Peter with the gospel of the circumcision.* Thus Paul resumes his interrupted thought and states in another form what he had begun to say in the first clause of the preceding verse; namely, that instead of correcting his doctrine, or of imparting to him any new truth, they had seen in his communication to them evidence of his having been commissioned to preach the glad tidings to the uncircumcised, and evidence as clear as they had of Peter's commission to preach the same glad tidings to the circumcised. For the word 'circumcision' stands for circumcised, the abstract for the concrete, and the word 'uncircumcision' for uncircumcised, in like manner.

8. For he that wrought effectually in Peter to the apostleship of the circumcision, the same was mighty in me toward the Gentiles. In this parenthetic sentence Paul assigns the reason why his communication was so convincing to those who heard it, and why they did not attempt to instruct him in regard to the gospel or concerning his work among the Gentiles. God, who had been with Peter, and had wrought for him, to make his ministry among the Jews effectual, had wrought as manifestly for Paul, to make effectual his mission and message to the heathen. Apostolic gifts had been imparted to both in perhaps equal measure. The Greek word employed is suggestive in the first place of spiritual influence, energizing the inward life, increasing faith, zeal, and courage. Indirectly it embraces also the outward signs and workings of that faith, everything, indeed, including miracles, by which God wrought for the apostles, and made their ministry effectual.

9. And when James, Cephas, and John, who seemed to be pillars, perceived the grace that was given unto me. The word translated 'saw' in ver. 7, refers, according to Ellicott, "to the mental impression produced, when the nature and success of St. Paul's preaching was brought before them"; and the word here translated 'perceived' refers to "the result of the actual information they derived from him." According to Lightfoot, the former word "describes the *apprehension* of the outward tokens of his commission, as evinced by his successful labors; the latter, the *conviction* arrived at in consequence, that the grace of God was with him. See 4: 8, 9." **They gave to me and Barnabas the right hands of fellowship.** In this verse James outranks Peter, though just before Peter is made the representative apostle of the circumcision. The prominence of James in this public expression of fellowship is explained by the fact that he was the pastor of the church at Jerusalem, and seems to have pre-

[1] According to the Revised Version the conjunction (γάρ) which introduces this clause is not causal but explicative; Boise says: "intensive and explicative"; and the best translation of it is 'I say.' See the article in Thayer's New Testament Lexicon under the word γάρ.

10 Only *they would* that we should remember the poor; the same which I also was forward to do.
11 But when Peter was come to Antioch, I withstood him to the face, because he was to be blamed.
12 For before that certain came from James, he did eat with the Gentiles: but when they were come, he withdrew and separated himself, fearing them which were of the circumcision.

10 only *they would* that we should remember the poor; which very thing I was also zealous to do.
11 But when Cephas came to Antioch, I resisted him to the face, because he stood condemned. For before that certain came from James, he did eat with the Gentiles: but when they came, he drew back and separated himself, fearing them that

sided at the public conferences. He would, therefore, naturally take precedence of Peter and John on this occasion, in the formal recognition of Paul as the chief apostle to the Gentiles. It is also noticeable that, in describing this visit to Jerusalem, Paul does not call James 'the brother of the Lord,' as he did in describing his first visit to Jerusalem (1:19); for James, the brother of John, was no longer alive, and the only James now prominent and likely to be thought of by his readers, was the brother of the Lord, known far and wide as the bishop at Jerusalem. Such apparently incidental agreement of language with historical fact is a striking proof of the authenticity of this letter. **That we should go unto the heathen** (*Gentiles*), **and they unto the circumcision**—that is, to the end, with the understanding that, 'we, to the Gentiles; and they, to the circumcision.' Whether the full expression would be 'should go,' or 'should be apostles,' is not perfectly certain. Of the main thought there can be no doubt. Paul and Barnabas were to give themselves chiefly to work for and among the Gentiles; James and Cephas and John were—at least, for the present—to give themselves to Christian labor for the Jews. But the understanding (it may be presumed) was not that either the one or the other should confine himself strictly to Gentiles, on the one hand, or to Jews, on the other. Neither is it to be supposed that this was an arrangement for life. It suited the existing state of the work, and might be expected to continue until new circumstances called for some modification of it.

10. Only they would that we should remember the poor, the same which I also was forward to do (*which very thing I was also zealous to do*)—that is, Paul, independently of their desire or request, was eager to render assistance, through the help of Gentile churches to the poor saints in Judea. See

Rom. 15 : 27; 1 Cor. 16 : 1, seq.; 2 Cor. 7 : 1, seq.; Acts 11 : 30, seq.; 24 : 17. The desire of the 'pillar apostles' that Paul and Barnabas should remember the poverty of the Jewish Christians, and render them charitable aid in time of need, shows their friendly feeling; for they would not have asked alms from any but friends.

11-21. PAUL'S REPROOF OF PETER AT ANTIOCH FOR HIS INCONSISTENT CONDUCT.

11. But when Peter (*Cephas*) **was come** (*came*) **to Antioch, I withstood** (*resisted*) **him to the face, because he was to be blamed** (*stood condemned*)—literally, *was condemned;* whether by the course which he had allowed himself to take, or by the judgment of the church, we cannot certainly affirm, but are inclined to the former view. Of the fact, however, that he had been and was condemned, there can be no doubt, as it is certified to us by the inspired apostle. And no one can be rightfully condemned who has not done wrong. The expression, 'resisted him to the face,' accords with all that is known of the openness, the courage, and the decision of Paul. Peter was, in some respects, the first of the apostles, a natural leader of men, a path breaker in evangelical work, and one highly esteemed by his brethren. It was, therefore, no easy task to oppose him face to face, because his conduct was inconsistent and disastrous. Yet Paul declares that he did this, and we have every reason to believe his statement strictly true. In the next verse he justifies his declaration that Peter was condemned as follows:

12. For before that certain came from James, he did eat with the Gentiles; but when they were come (*came*),[1] **he withdrew** (*drew back*) **and separated himself, fearing them which** (*that*) **were of the circumcision.** By such conduct, whatever he may have thought of it himself, or what-

---

[1] Several early documents (viz., א B D * F G, with Origen and a few cursives) read, " but when he (that is, James) came "—ὅτε δὲ ἦλθεν ; but this is a reading which even Westcott and Hort pronounces "unquestionably wrong," though supported by א B, a combination which is usually very strong, yet, in the present case, weakened by the 'Western' documents D * G.

13 And the other Jews dissembled likewise with him; insomuch that Barnabas also was carried away with their dissimulation.

14 But when I saw that they walked not uprightly according to the truth of the gospel, I said unto Peter before *them* all, If thou, being a Jew, livest after the

13 were of the circumcision. And the rest of the Jews dissembled likewise with him; insomuch that even Barnabas was carried away with their dissimulation.

14 tion. But when I saw that they walked not uprightly according to the truth of the gospel, I said unto Cephas before *them* all, If thou, being

ever the people may have said of it, Peter was condemned. The expression 'certain from James' may signify that the persons in question were sent by him to Antioch, or that they came from the church of which he was the bishop, and professed to represent his opinion. But from all we know of his steadiness of mind, it would be unjust to suspect him of authorizing the course pursued by these Judaists. 'Did eat with the Gentiles'—that is to say, was eating with them, or was in the habit of eating with them; the verb being in the imperfect tense. The Greek verbs rendered, 'drew back and separated himself,' describe his action in progress and at completion. He seems to have broken off his free intercourse with Gentiles somewhat gradually and reluctantly, but at last the separation was the same as that between ordinary Jews and Gentiles. Yet observe that he did not do this of his own accord—he did it rather through his fear of losing the good will and confidence of the Jewish brethren, represented by those who had come there from Jerusalem, and who doubtless had said a great deal about the Jewish manner of life for which James is reported to have been conspicuous. "It is remarkable," says Prof. Jowett, "and may be considered as a proof of the truth of the history, that his conduct, however unintelligible, is in keeping with Peter's character. We recognize in it the lineaments of him who confessed Christ first, and first denied him; who began by refusing that Christ should wash his feet, and then said, "not my feet only, but my hands and my head"; who cut off the ear of the servant of the high priest, when they came to take Jesus, and then forsook him and fled. Boldness and timidity—first boldness, then timidity—were the characteristics of his nature." But the matter did not end with Peter's withdrawal. Others followed his example.

13. And the other Jews (*the rest of the Jews*) **dissembled likewise with him: insomuch that Barnabas also** (or, *even Barnabas*) **was carried away with their dissimulation.** Thus the weight of Peter's

example, added to the urgency of their kinsmen from the mother church, led the other Christian Jews of Antioch to separate themselves from the Gentiles, though they, as well as Peter, did this against their better judgment. There is no evidence that Peter solicited them to take this course. It is even possible that he yielded with many a protest to the Judaizing faction. But that he yielded at all, was a fact that could be used with tremendous effect by zealots for the law, and for a brief period it seemed as if a great wave of Jewish ritualism were about to sweep away the old landmarks of the church, as if the form of godliness were to take the place of its power, and pretense get the upper hand of sincerity. The second part of the verse shows how powerful was the Judaistic current. 'Even Barnabas,' the fast friend and enlightened companion of Paul, was carried away by it. He was the last man to be moved in that direction, and the circumstance that even he was swept along with the rest, though reluctantly, shows that a crisis had been reached in the church. But by the good providence of God there was on the ground a 'Hebrew of the Hebrews' whose grasp of principles, and foresight of consequences, and courage in asserting the truth, were equal to the emergency. It was for him to wrest the victory from those who must have thought themselves to be already in full possession of the field.

14. But when I saw that they walked not uprightly according to the truth of the gospel, I said unto Peter (*Cephas*) before them all. Lightfoot explains the first part of this verse by saying, "they diverge from the straight path of the gospel truth." "The preposition translated 'according to' (πρὸς) here denotes not the goal to be attained, but the line of direction to be observed." The reasons why Paul took occasion to reprove Peter before the whole church were doubtless these: that Peter's offense was in some sense public, that its bad influence could be averted in no other way, and that many had dissembled with him and needed reproof as well as he. Both Jews and Gentiles

manner of Gentiles, and not as do the Jews, why compellest thou the Gentiles to live as do the Jews?

15 We *who are* Jews by nature, and not sinners of the Gentiles,

16 Knowing that a man is not justified by the works of the law, but by the faith of Jesus Christ, even we have believed in Jesus Christ, that we might be justified by the faith of Christ, and not by the works of the law; for by the works of the law shall no flesh be justified.

a Jew, livest as do the Gentiles, and not as do the Jews, how compellest thou the Gentiles to live 15 as do the Jews? We being Jews by nature, and 16 not sinners of the Gentiles, yet knowing that a man is not justified by [1] the works of the law, but through faith in Jesus Christ, even we believed on Christ Jesus, that we might be justified by faith in Christ, and not by the works of the law: because by the works of the law shall no flesh be justified.

1 Or, *works of law.*

must be made to see that not even this great apostle's example could be safely followed when it was inconsistent with the gospel. If the remedy applied by Paul was drastic, it was without doubt needed and effectual. Having the consciences of believing Jews and Gentiles in Antioch on his side, a public method of dealing with the matter was safe and wise; at any rate, it was in keeping with his own character as revealed to us by the New Testament.

We now come to the address itself, which appears to be rehearsed by the apostle in a condensed form, but with substantial accuracy. A few years, it is true (possibly six or seven), had passed since he made it, but the occasion was so exigent and the effect of his words so important that they must have been often recalled by him with thankfulness to God for the grace which enabled him to speak them. Moreover, we are justified in believing that the Spirit of inspiration co-operated with natural circumstances in making his memory faithful. **If thou, being a Jew, livest after the manner of the Gentiles, and not as do the Jews, why compellest thou the Gentiles to live as do the Jews?** This direct appeal to the inconsistency of Peter's conduct could only be met by confessing that he had done wrong in living as do the Gentiles, or by confessing that he was wrong in refusing to live thus, when his refusal would sanction the efforts of the Judaizing party, and would by so much tend to compel the Gentile believers to live as Jews, for the sake of unity and peace. When Paul speaks of Peter as living (present tense) like the Gentiles, he refers to his recent and well-known practice; and he is able to do this with all the more confidence because the principles of Peter would require him to live "ethnically" whenever his apostolic work called for it. It is easy to imagine the consternation which stole into the hearts of 'certain from James,'

when they heard these words and recollected Peter's visit to Cornelius, his account of the sheet let down from heaven, his speech at the so-called council, and his intercourse with the Gentile converts before their own arrival in Antioch. Perhaps they began at that moment to see that they had not counted the cost when they undertook to overturn Paul's work in Antioch. His bold and strong words must at least have gone to the conscience of Peter. But Peter was of so true and noble a spirit that he could bear reproof and listen to argument as well.

After this *argumentum ad hominem*, Paul courteously associates himself with Peter, when it would have been just as easy for him to have continued his address in the second person singular. A little below, with the same spirit of courtesy, he passes to the first person singular. (Ver. 18.)

15-16. We who are (literally, *we being*) **Jews by nature, and not sinners of the Gentiles,** (*yet*) **knowing that a man is not justified by the works of the law, but** (*save*) **by** (*through*) **faith in Jesus Christ, even we believed in Jesus Christ, that we might be justified by the faith of** (*in*) **Christ, and not by the works of the law: for** (*because*) **by the works of the law no flesh shall be justified.** The first clause is concessive: 'Although we were Jews by birth, and not heathen-born sinners'; the second is causal, 'yet because we knew that a man is not justified by the works of the law, but only through faith'; the third is declarative, 'even we believed on Christ Jesus'; the fourth is final, to the end 'that we might be justified by the faith in Christ, and not by the works of the law'; and the fifth confirmatory, 'because by the works of the law shall no flesh (or, sinful man) be justified.' There seems at first sight to be some needless repetition in this verse, but, strictly speaking, there is none; the fullness of statement in every

17 But if, while we seek to be justified by Christ, we ourselves also are found sinners, is therefore Christ the minister of sin? God forbid.

14 For if I build again the things which I destroyed, I make myself a transgressor.

15 For I through the law am dead to the law, that I might live unto God.

17 But if, while we sought to be justified in Christ, we ourselves also were found sinners, is Christ a minister of sin? God forbid. For if I build up again

18 those things which I destroyed, I prove myself a

19 transgressor. For I through ¹ the law died unto

¹ Or, law.

clause is emphatic. It is, however, to be observed that the last sentence, 'because by the deeds of the law shall no flesh be justified,' is inserted as an Old Testament proof of the preceding clause. It is probably a free citation of Ps. 143 : 2, which reads thus: "And enter not into judgment with thy servant; for in thy sight shall no man living be justified." Paul introduces the words, 'by the deeds of the law,' on the assumption that when God is said in the Old Testament to 'enter into judgment' with any one, the law must be the standard, obedience to the whole law the only ground of justification, and disobedience to any part of it a sufficient ground of condemnation. To keep the law is to keep the whole of it; to break the law is to disobey any command of it. It may also be remarked that the meaning of the apostle in the sentence, 'a man is not justified by the works of the law, but (ἐὰν μὴ) through faith,' is correctly represented in English by translating the Greek (ἐὰν μὴ, seq.) 'but only' through faith in Jesus Christ. The whole statement may then be reproduced as follows: 'Although we were Jews by birth, and not heathen-born sinners, yet because we knew that a man is not justified by the works of the law, but only through faith in Jesus Christ, even we, I say, believed on Christ Jesus, in order that we might be justified by faith in Christ, and not by works which the law requires; because by the works of the law (as it is written) shall no flesh be justified.' Compare Rom. 3 : 20. Thus Paul assumes, as a fact which Peter will admit, that both of them had turned away in despair from legal works as a condition of acceptance with God, and had put their trust in Christ alone. Let us now see what use he makes of this unquestionable fact.

17. But if, while we seek (sought) to be justified by (in) Christ, we ourselves also are (were) found sinners, is therefore Christ the (a) minister of sin? God forbid! It cannot for a moment be supposed, argues Paul, that in and by our seeking to be jus-

tified by Christ, without the works of the law, we also ourselves, as these sticklers for the law affirm, were found in the way of sin and on a plane with the Gentiles, for then it would follow that Christ is 'a minister' and promoter of sin; a conclusion abhorrent to every believer! We did not then break the law and commit sin by looking to Christ alone for acceptance with God, although in doing this we ceased to keep the law as a means of justification. Just the opposite of this is true. **For if I build (up) again the things which I destroyed, I make (prove) myself a transgressor.** In this verse the apostle substitutes, with great delicacy of feeling, the first person singular for the first person plural. For the act supposed was precisely that for which Peter stood condemned. What he had been doing by his example was a building up again of legal observances, which he had before destroyed by testifying that they were no longer obligatory on Christians as the ground of justification, and were means of condemnation rather than of justification. The true purpose of the law was to convince men of sin and drive them away from itself to Christ. Hence those who turn back to legal works as a condition of forgiveness and life, transgress the very nature and purpose of the law. This thought is explained and justified by the next verse. Apart from that verse, we might be in doubt respecting the import of this, but with it the meaning of this is perfectly clear.

19. For I through the law am dead (died) to the law, that I might live unto God. The emphatic words are 'through the law.' "It was the law itself, doing its appointed work, by which I was slain to the law—that is, driven from it and made utterly dead to it as a means of salvation. It refused me hope; it said, 'To rely upon me is to perish; thou hast sinned, and the soul that sinneth shall die; trust me not, but flee to the mercy of God in Christ.' Thus by the proper action of the law I was made to relinquish all my confidence in it as a means of justification

c

20 I am crucified with Christ: nevertheless I live; yet not I, but Christ liveth in me: and the life which I now live in the flesh I live by the faith of the Son of God, who loved me, and gave himself for me.

20 ¹ the law, that I might live unto God. I have been crucified with Christ; and it is no longer I that live, but Christ liveth in me: and that *life* which I now live in the flesh I live in faith, *the faith* which is in the Son of God, who loved me, and gave him-

1 Or, *law.*

before God. By its own impulsion I turned from it and ceased to have any life-relation to it, but in this very act I turned to Christ in faith, to the end that I might enter upon a new and true life, a life which is closely related to God, is sustained by his grace, and is consecrated to his service." This appears to be the import of the apostle's language in the present verse, and it fully explains and confirms the preceding verse.

Paul has now reached the core of the gospel, as understood and preached by him; and so he must needs dwell upon it a moment longer. For surely this, if anything, will reach the heart of his brother Cephas, and prevail upon him to give up the attempt to build again what he has once destroyed.

20. I am (*have been*) **crucified with Christ.** Nothing is deeper in the writings of Paul than his conception of the believer's union with Christ. He dies to the law and to sin by trusting in Christ. His legal standing and his spiritual condition are reversed in a moment by that act and the union which depends upon it. In the preceding verse, and also in this, the reference is chiefly to the former, yet the latter is doubtless involved. Paul's crucifixion with Christ was first realized at his conversion, but the continuance of that crucifixion had been experienced by him all along from that hour to the present. Essentially the same thought is repeated by the apostle in his letter to the Romans: "Knowing this, that our old man was crucified with him, that the body of sin might be done away, that so we should no longer live in bondage to sin; for he that hath died is justified from sin." (6:6.) Compare also Rom. 6:8; Gal. 5:24; 6:14; Col. 2:20, and Rom 6:4; Col. 2:12. Translate: *And it is no longer I that live, but Christ liveth in me.* That is, I have no longer a separate existence, for Christ is the life of my life. He is its source, its animating principle, its object. "For to me to live is Christ." (Phil. 1:21.) "When Christ, who is our life, shall be manifested," etc. (Col. 3:4.) "I am the vine, ye are the branches." (John 15:5.) "I in them, and thou

in me, that they may be perfected into one." (John 17:23.) There must be something very real and wonderful to justify such language: a union of Christ with his people which can only be described by saying that his life pervades their life, giving it power and purity and peace not its own. **And the life which I now live in the flesh.** The word 'flesh' is here equivalent to body, and life in the body is conceived to be a life exposed to weakness and temptation—a life of toil, of conflict, and perhaps of persecution—a life which will fail of the highest good, unless it be to him who is empowered by the Divine Spirit in the inner man, and looks "not at the things which are seen, but at the things which are not seen." (2 Cor. 4:18.) Such a man was the apostle. He was in the flesh, but not the servant of it; for he said, "I buffet my body, and bring it into bondage: lest by any means, after that I have preached to others, I myself should be rejected." (1 Cor. 9:27.) **I live by** (*in*) **the faith of** (*which is in*) **the Son of God, who loved me, and gave himself** (*up*) **for me.** Faith was the element in which Paul was living and breathing, and that faith had for its object the Son of God. In him the apostle trusted, and not in his own righteousness; in the Son of God, and not in legal observances, or holy resolutions, or perfected character. He expected salvation as a free gift through a Divine Saviour. The last clause, 'who loved me and gave himself up for me,' is a pathetic and grateful recognition of Christ's voluntary death for the redemption of sinners, and of the holy impulse which moved him to so great a sacrifice. At the same time it shows how tender and personal was the relation of Jesus to the apostle, if we accept the apostle's view of that relation. Blessed must this sorely-tried servant of Christ have been when he uttered this sentence, and believed that it would be as dear to the heart of Peter as to his own! And having said this, he closes with a declaration and a reason for it; both of which relate to the controversy about Jewish observances as a condition of acceptance with God.

21 I do not frustrate the grace of God: for if righteousness *come* by the law, then Christ is dead in vain.

21 self up for me. I do not make void the grace of
God: for if righteousness is through [1] the law, then
Christ died for nought.

1 Or, *law.*

21. I do not frustrate (*make void*) **the grace of God**—as do those who insist upon obedience to the Jewish Law as a condition of salvation; **for if righteousness come by** (*is through*) **the law, then Christ is dead in vain** (*died for nought*). Evidently Paul assumes that a falling back upon legal works for justification or righteousness is radically inconsistent with justification through faith in Christ. It must be one thing or the other: a combination of the two is out of the question. If a man can be justified by the law, he needs no Saviour. If he needs Christ at all, it is because he is condemned by the law. Observe how closely the death of Christ and the grace of God are here connected. To reject one is to reject the other. Indeed, the death of Christ is esteemed by the apostle the grandest expression of God's grace, and anything which proclaims this death unnecessary is a thorough denial of God's grace in human salvation. There is much reason to believe that Peter was convinced of his mistake by this address of Paul, and that he never fell into the same again. And, though we may regret his timid yielding to Jewish zealots at this time, we cannot be too thankful that Paul was on the ground to maintain the truth in its purity. The narrative has always been troublesome to Roman Catholics, because it shows so clearly the weakness of Peter and his being subject to correction by Paul. To talk of him as prince of the apostles and head of all the church in presence of this piece of history requires vast assurance. Hence, this is by no means a favorite passage with Roman Catholic writers, and some of them have made desperate attempts to discover in it some other meaning than it obviously contains. But its meaning is indubitable. Peter did in this case, as once before, yield to fear, and do what he could not approve. This must be conceded, though with reluctance, by Romanist and Protestant: with reluctan e by the Romanist, because it disagrees with his doctrine of the rectoral supremacy of Peter in the college of the apostles and in the whole militant church; and with reluctance by the Protestant also, be-

cause it seems incompatible with the highest apostolic inspiration. To reconcile this episode in Peter's life with the Papal theory of his being the vicar of Christ on earth seems impossible, but a few things may be said of its bearing on the doctrine of apostolical inspiration.

First, the circumstance may be recalled, that in the articles of pacification, adopted at Jerusalem a few weeks before, nothing was said in respect to the intercourse of Jewish converts with Gentiles. The Holy Spirit seems to have waited for certain events to take place before revealing to Jewish believers the impropriety and danger to Christian life which a permanent observance of the Mosaic ritual involved. He foresaw that the destruction of the temple would at no distant day fill their minds with serious questions as to the duty or possibility of preserving intact their ancestral customs. And there is reason to suppose that not much instruction was given them respecting the evils of their caste system of religious life till they were providentially qualified to receive it kindly. Even Paul, who was perfectly aware of the danger of clinging to legal rites as a condition of acceptance with God, was willing to live as a Jew with Jews for the sake of gaining them for Christ. He knew, indeed, as did Peter and Barnabas also, that it was right for Jews to mingle freely with Gentiles in the service of Jesus, but it does not appear that he or they had been led by the Spirit of God to protest against the course of James and of many others in keeping the law. This must be duly considered in forming an estimate of Peter's conduct.

Secondly, Peter is not represented as saying anything in justification of his conduct, or against free social intercourse on the part of Jews with Gentiles. He seems to have yielded to pressure in so far as his action was concerned, but he may have hoped to gain the Judaizers by temporary concessions. He may have said to them: "I go with you, because my mission is to you rather than to the Gentiles, but I do not admit the correctness of

CHAPTER III.

O FOOLISH Galatians, who hath bewitched you, that ye should not obey the truth, before whose eyes Jesus Christ hath been evidently set forth, crucified among you?

1 O foolish Galatians, who did bewitch you, before whose eyes Jesus Christ was openly set forth crucified.

your position, or concede that it was wrong for me to eat with Gentiles; and I expect that you will soon look at the matter as I do!" Such a course may have seemed to Cephas almost necessary, at least for a time, and the far-reaching consequences of it may have been overlooked by him until Paul brought them to mind.

Thirdly, from this instance, as well as from the history of the ancient prophets in Israel, it is evident that divine inspiration was never meant to insure a perfect life to its possessor. There is but one such life described in the New Testament, and none in the Old. Somewhere, then, a line must be drawn between teaching and conduct, and it must be conceded that a man may be enabled to deliver a true message from God, though his knowledge and his life are imperfect.

Fourthly, it is worth while to remember that God's providence is a factor of history. A man was then present in Antioch by the will of God who could meet the emergency in such a way that even Peter's dissimulation was overruled for good. Humanly considered, it was just the place and the time for this occurrence. A great and hitherto unsettled question could now be answered in such a manner as to satisfy the Gentiles, if not the Jews. It was thus answered in strict agreement with the spirit and genius of Christianity. If the divine hand is ever discernible in human affairs, it is in this sad but important transaction at Antioch. And it was a transaction, the recital of which could not fail to impress upon the Galatians the high authority of Paul as a Christian teacher, and the perfect clearness and truth of his gospel. It introduced, therefore, in a most effective manner the argument which he was about to make in support of the doctrine of salvation by the grace of God through faith in Christ.

Ch. 3: In support of his gospel, that justification is of grace through faith, Paul now appeals:

1. To their Experience of the Grace of God through Faith in Christ Crucified. (1-5.)—"Having thus, in the first two chapters, vindicated his authority as an apostle, or, in other words, shown that the gospel which he preached must be true, because he was taught it by direct revelation, Paul proceeds in the next place to argue the truth of this gospel, from a consideration of the system, both as viewed in itself and as attested by the appropriate external marks of its divine character. A summary of the argument as developed in this connection is the following: The gratuitous system of justification as contained in the gospel must be the true one in opposition to that of merit or works; first, because the Holy Spirit accompanies its reception as a witness that those who embrace it are the children of God (ver. 2-4); second, because it has been sanctioned by miracles (ver. 5); third, because it accords with the manner in which Abraham was justified (ver. 6, 7); fourth, because it fulfills the predictions of the Old Testament, which declare that Christ was to be the medium through which spiritual blessing should be conferred on mankind (ver. 8, 9); fifth, because it agrees with the entire teaching of the Old Testament in regard to the justifying power of faith (ver. 11); and, finally, because it is the only system adapted to men as sinners."

"In confirmation of this last point, it is shown that on the ground of obedience justification is impossible, because the obedience which the law demands must be perfect; and as no individual renders this, it is evident that as many as are of the law are under the curse. Under these circumstances, therefore, Christ gave himself as a ransom to redeem us from the curse of the law, being made himself a curse for us, and thus providing a way of salvation which is applicable to all, Gentiles as well as Jews, on condition of faith. (ver. 10, 12-14.)" (Hackett.)

1. O foolish Galatians, who hath bewitched you, etc. By these words Paul resumes his direct appeal to the Galatians. Having vindicated his claim to be an apostle, instructed by Christ himself through revelation, and recognized as their peer by the elder

2 This only would I learn of you, Received ye the Spirit by the works of the law, or by the hearing of faith?
3 Are ye so foolish? having begun in the Spirit, are ye now made perfect by the flesh?

2 fied? This only would I learn from you, Received ye the Spirit by [1] the works of the law, or by the [2] hearing of faith? Are ye so foolish? having begun in

1 Or, works of law......2 Or, message.

apostles, he is brought, by the repetition of his protest and argument against Peter's course in Antioch, to the deepest ground of his opposition to the Judaistic error, which is, that it nullifies the grace of God by virtually pronouncing Christ's death unnecessary. So irrational does this appear to the deeply moved apostle, that he cannot refrain from great plainness of speech in addressing the Galatians. Their course suggests the influence of such fascination as is popularly attributed to "the evil eye." It is a surprising, unaccountable course, especially when the apostle recalls the clearness with which he had portrayed to them the atoning death of Christ.[1]

Before whose eyes Jesus Christ hath been evidently (was openly) set forth crucified?—that is, was portrayed as crucified. The word translated 'was openly set forth' (προεγράφη) is used to remind them of the clear and vivid manner in which Paul had delineated the death of Christ; and the word 'crucified' (ἐσταυρωμενος), placed for the sake of emphasis at the end of the sentence, is used to recall the dreadful character of that death. The language of this clause is interesting as giving a hint of the "matter and manner" of Paul's preaching. In Galatia, as well as in Corinth, the substance of his message was, 'Jesus Christ, and him crucified.' See 1 Cor. 1 : 23, seq. And his manner, it cannot be doubted, was bold, earnest, impassioned, and often tender. (Act. 20 : 31.) The question of this verse, indicating so much surprise and sorrow, is followed by other questions which show the reasons for his surprise at the irrationality of their conduct. They bring out the inconsistency and folly of it in striking language.

2. This only would I learn of (from) you. As if the answer to the single question he was about to propose would be conclusive of the whole matter. **Received ye the**

Spirit by (the) works of (the) law or by (the) hearing of faith? The preposition translated 'by' signifies out of, as a result of, or, by means of. In this place it is properly rendered 'by,' in the sense of, by means of. The noun which is translated 'hearing' is also used to denote organ of hearing, or ear, and what is heard, whether it be instruction or rumor. Hence, it is an open question whether Paul describes them as having received the Holy Spirit by hearkening to the good news with faith, or by means of preaching, which related to faith as the condition of justification. In either case the emphasis falls upon faith as contrasted with works. And as he appeals to their own experience, it is almost certain that the works of the Holy Spirit had been so marked at the time of their conversion—and, probably, afterward—as to be easily perceived by them and distinguished from everything else in their inner life. It is likewise probable that many of them had been endowed with special gifts by the Spirit of God, as those of prophecy, speaking with tongues, or miracles. Of course, the apostle conceives of but one answer as possible to the question proposed. They had received the Spirit by listening with faith to the gospel of Christ. This was certain to him, and, in his opinion, certain to them as well.

3. Are ye so foolish? Namely, as the next question is about to suggest. In the New Testament, the adverb 'so' (οὕτως) often points to what follows. **Having begun in the Spirit, are ye now made perfect by the flesh?** Compare 2 Cor. 8 : 6; Phil. 1 : 6. Perhaps the middle sense of the verb is preferable, 'Are ye now making an end in the flesh?' "Having made a beginning in Christianity, are ye now making an end in Judaism?" (Boise.) One becomes a Christian, not by natural birth, but by spiritual birth. "That which is born of the flesh is flesh, and that

[1] The words 'that ye should not obey the truth' must be rejected as forming no part of the original text. They are wanting in N A B D * F G P, and some of the best cursives. Lightfoot conjectures that they were added from Gal. 5 : 7. They are omitted by Tischendorf, Tregelles, Westcott and Hort, and the Revised Version.

4 Have ye suffered so many things in vain? if *it be* yet in vain.

5 He therefore that ministereth to you the Spirit, and worketh miracles among you, *doth he it* by the works of the law, or by the hearing of faith?

4 the Spirit,[1] are ye now perfected in the flesh? Did ye suffer so many things in vain? if it be indeed in

5 vain. He therefore who supplieth to you the Spirit, and worketh [2] miracles [3] among you, *doeth he it* by [4] the works of the law, or by the [5] hearing of faith?

---

1 Or, *do ye now make an end in the flesh?*....2 Or. *powers.*...3 Or, *in.*...4 Or. *works of law.*...5 Or, *message.*

---

which is born of the Spirit is spirit." (John 3 : 6.) 'In the Spirit' refers to the element in which the new life of the Christian has its beginning now, as well as in the first age. But the Jewish rites, which the Galatians were urged to observe as necessary to salvation, were carnal ordinances, intended to be superseded by the heart worship of a more spiritual economy.

4. Have ye suffered so many things in vain?—or, according to the Revised Version, *'Did ye suffer?'* etc. Just what sufferings for Christ's sake these Galatian disciples may have borne we do not know. But the pertinency and force of the apostle's question depend upon their severity. Light sufferings would not have suggested such an appeal. Their liberty in Christ must have been purchased at no small cost of afflictions. And the apostle calls upon them to consider the question whether they are ready to look upon their endurance of wrong in the past as useless. Had they been following a "will o' the wisp" into all manner of distress ever since they received the gospel and put their trust in Christ? The pertinence of this question would be more obvious still if a large part of their sufferings had been due to Jewish enmity against Christians—an enmity which they would not have provoked if they had kept the Jewish law.

Many give to the word translated 'have suffered' the meaning *'have experienced,'* and understand 'many things' to signify blessings. This interpretation suits the context perfectly; and the verb certainly has this meaning sometimes in classical Greek. But, aside from this passage, it never has that meaning in the New Testament, and hence we hesitate to fall back upon it here. **If it be yet** (or, *indeed*) **in vain**—'As your attitude toward Judaism seems now to affirm!' Yet there is also suggested by this clause a half-hidden hope that the fruit of their sufferings will not be lost by their actual adoption of the Judaistic error. Paul leaves the path open to a return to the way of life which they had formerly entered with joy in the Lord. The meaning of this clause is admitted to be obscure, but that which we have stated is more obvious than any other, and it agrees with the course of thought in this part of the apostle's argument. Lightfoot's note is striking.[1]

5. He therefore that ministereth to you the Spirit, or *that supplieth to you the Spirit.* The apostle now returns to the thought of ver. 2 and 3, from which he has deviated for an instant that he might refer to their heroic sufferings on account of fidelity to the truth. But even that deviation was merely formal, if we suppose that he regarded, and expected his readers to regard, their endurance of sufferings as a fruit of the Spirit's work in their hearts, giving them strength to bear affliction with joy. According to this view, the conjunction 'therefore' is resumptive, or, perhaps more exactly, as Ellicott remarks of the original word (οὖν), "*continuative* and *retrospective* rather than illative." Every interpreter knows that in the Gospel of John the same word (οὖν) is frequently translated 'then' instead of 'therefore,' because the sentences introduced by it do not appear to be in any obvious sense inferences from that which precedes them. So here the sense would be clearly expressed by translating: 'He then who is supplying to you the Spirit,' etc. **And worketh miracles among you** (or, *in you*). The ambiguity of the last words cannot be certainly removed by anything in the preceding language or in the context. They may signify 'in you' or 'among you,' though there is a slight presumption in favor of the former, as giving the ordinary meaning of the preposition, if the sense of the passage thus rendered is equally satisfactory. For

---

[1] 'If it be really in vain.' It is hard to believe this; the apostle hopes better things of his converts. Εἰ γε leaves a loophole for doubt, and καὶ widens this, implying an unwillingness to believe on the part of the speaker. The alternative rendering, 'If it is only in vain, and not worse than in vain,' seems harsh and improbable.

6 Even as Abraham believed God, and it was accounted to him for righteousness.
7 Know ye therefore that they which are of faith,
the same are the children of Abraham.

6 Even as Abraham believed God, and it was reckoned
7 unto him for righteousness. ¹ Know therefore that
they who are of faith, the same are sons of Abraham.

1 Or, Ye perceive.

'worketh miracles in you,' see 1 Cor. 12 :
28 and Matt. 14 : 2. Thus understood,
Paul must refer to spiritual gifts, such as
speaking with tongues, interpretation of
tongues, discerning of spirits, prophesying,
and the like, which were bestowed by the
Holy Spirit according to his own will. Yet
bodily cures of an extraordinary character in
answer to prayer might perhaps be described in
these terms. If, however, the versions are
correct in translating the words 'among you,'
the principal reference may be to miracles in
the world of sense, though others would not
of necessity be excluded. At all events, the
apostle here appeals to miracles as unquestionable facts in the history of the Galatian
churches, and founds upon them an argument against the Judaistic teaching, that men
could not be acceptable to God through faith
in Christ, without obeying the Jewish Law.

Doeth he it by the works of the law, or
by the hearing of faith? The subject of the
whole sentence is without any doubt God, and
the manifest assumption of the apostle is, that
the gift of the Holy Spirit to the Galatians,
and his marvelous working in them, had depended in no degree on their obedience to
the Jewish Law, but altogether on their faith
in Christ. Indeed, there is no evidence that
they had yet observed the Jewish rites to any
considerable extent, or, if any of them had done
this, Paul was certain that they could not ascribe this working of the Holy Spirit in them
or among them to their legal works. Hence he
presses the question boldly as one that must
receive an answer which would refute all possible arguments for keeping the law as a condition of justification with God.

2. CONFIRMATION OF THIS VIEW BY AN
APPEAL TO THE BIBLE ACCOUNT OF ABRA-
HAM'S JUSTIFICATION. (6-9.)

6. Even as Abraham believed God, and
it was accounted (reckoned) to him for
righteousness. The answer of the previous
question is left to be supplied by the reader.
It must be: 'surely of faith,' and with this in
mind the apostle adds : 'Even as Abraham
believed God,' etc. The phraseology of the

quotation is borrowed from the Septuagint
Version of Gen. 15 : 6, which, however, fairly
reproduces the sense of the Hebrew original.
That original is translated in the Canterbury
Revision : "And he believed in the Lord, and
he counted it to him for righteousness." The
same passage is quoted by the apostle in his
Epistle to the Romans (4 : 3) with the important
comment : "Now to him that worketh, the
reward is not reckoned as of grace, but as of
debt. But to him that worketh not, but believeth on him that justifieth the ungodly,
his faith is reckoned for righteousness."
(Ver. 4 and 5.) Clearly, then, according to Paul,
Abraham's faith was accepted by God, in
place of righteousness, or a perfect life, as a
condition of justification. "Because of this
faith in Christ," says Martin Luther, "God
seeth not my doubting of his good-will toward
me, my distrust, heaviness of spirit, and other
sins which are yet in me. For as long as I live
in the flesh, sin is truly in me. But because I am
covered under the shadow of Christ's wings,
as is the chicken under the wing of the hen,
and dwell without fear under that most ample
and large heaven of the forgiveness of sins,
which is spread over me, God covereth and
pardoneth the remnant of sin in me—that is
to say, because of that faith wherewith I began
to lay hold upon Christ, he accepteth my imperfect righteousness even for perfect righteousness, and counteth my sin for no sin, which
notwithstanding is sin indeed."

7. Know ye therefore that they which
are of faith, the same are the children of
Abraham. With equal propriety the verse
may be rendered : Ye know therefore that they
who are of faith, these are sons of Abraham.
The word 'these' is emphatic, these and no
others. Though the imperative 'know' is more
animated than the indicative 'ye know' or
perceive, it seems less natural in a passage so
argumentative as this has now become. The
readers are presumed to see that only persons
of the same religious spirit as Abraham can be
properly called his sons. Compare the same
apostle's words in Rom. 4:11, seq., and the Saviour's words in John 8:8, 39. Lightfoot explains

8 And the Scripture, forseeing that God would justify the heathen through faith, preached before the gospel unto Abraham, *saying*, In thee shall all nations be blessed.
9 So then they which be of faith are blessed with faithful Abraham.

8 And the scripture, foreseeing that God [1] would justify the [2] Gentiles by faith, preached the gospel beforehand unto Abraham, *saying*, In thee shall all the 9 nations be blessed. So then they who are of faith

1 Gr. *justifieth*......2 Gr. *nations*.

the phrase 'who are of faith' (οἱ ἐκ πίστεως) as meaning, "they whose starting-point, whose fundamental principle is faith," and Sieffert-Meyer says that it "designates the believers according to their specific peculiarity genetically. Faith is that from which their spiritual condition springs. Compare Rom. 2: 8; 3: 26; 4: 14; John 18: 37."

8. And the Scripture, foreseeing that God would justify the heathen through faith, the Gentiles by faith. 'The Scripture' is here personified as having divine foresight, doubtless because it is conceived of as being the word, and therefore, virtually, the intelligence of God. Compare Rom. 4: 3, 9, 17; John 7: 38, where it is spoken of as saying that which God says in and by it. The verb 'would justify' is in the present tense to denote the rule of action fixed in the mind of God and followed by him. And the words 'by faith' are emphatic, containing the principal thought of the participial clause. **Preached before the gospel unto Abraham.** See Revised Version. Of course, it was God, whose words were subsequently recorded and are preserved in Scripture, who did this. In the personification, the Scripture is simply said to do what God, the Supreme Author of it, really did. **Saying, In thee shall all (*the*) nations be blessed.** "That promise was an evangel before the evangel." (Sieffert.) It is to be found in Gen. 12: 3, according to the Septuagint, though the apostle has substituted 'all the nations' for 'all the families of the earth.' In Gen. 18: 18 the same promise is repeated with reference to Abraham: "And all the nations of the earth shall be blessed in him." The precise sense of 'in thee' cannot be easily fixed. Lightfoot says: "'In thee,' as their spiritual father"; but we ask, In what sense is Abraham the spiritual father of believing Gentiles? Ellicott says a little more: "'In thee' as the spiritual father of all the faithful, —the preposition with its usual force specifying Abraham as the *substratum, foundation*, on which, and in which, the blessing rests.

Compare 1 Cor. 7: 14." But this seems to put Abraham very nearly in the place which Paul everywhere else assigns to Christ. Sieffert remarks: "'In thee,' that is, in this fact, that thou art blessed, is contained (as a consequence) the being blessed of all the heathen, in so far, namely, as all the heathen were to attain through faith to justification and through justification to the reception of the Holy Spirit, but in the blessing of Abraham, the father of all believers (Rom. 4), the connection of faith and justification was revealed and established for all future time." This is better. Jowett thinks that 'in thee' is equivalent to "in thee as their type," or "in thy faith," adding that "the general meaning is as follows: It was not a mere accident that it was said, 'In thee shall all the Gentiles be blessed'; but because Abraham was justified by faith, as the Gentiles were to be justified by faith." It may then be sufficient to say that Abraham was the primary and palmary example of justification by faith, in whom were made known to mankind the principle and condition on which all men in subsequent ages were to find acceptance with God. Therefore all who resemble him in faith are called his sons, and their justification is conceived of as but a repetition or amplification of his. There does not appear to be any explicit reference to Christ in the word 'thee'; that reference is to be found in the added words of ver. 16, "thy seed."

9. So then they which (*that*) be of faith are blessed with faithful Abraham. Here, by way of general conclusion, Paul affirms that believers are blessed with the believing Abraham. 'With Abraham' the apostle now writes, not 'in him'; by which the joint participation in the blessing of God on the same terms is simply and strongly affirmed. The spiritual attitude toward God which was acceptable in the case of Abraham is acceptable in every man, whether Jew or Gentile. Compare Rom. 4: 23.

Paul has now appealed, (*a*) to the early ex-

10 For as many as are of the works of the law are under the curse: for it is written, Cursed is every one that continueth not in all things which are written in the book of the law to do them.

10 are blessed with the faithful Abraham. For as many as are of 1 the works of the law are under a curse: for it is written, Cursed is every one who continueth not in all things that are written in the book of the

1 Or. works of law.

perience which the Galatians enjoyed of the Holy Spirit's work in their hearts, (b) to the great sufferings which they had been enabled to bear for Christ's sake, and (c) to the extraordinary spiritual gifts which they had received—all coming to them through faith in Christ, without the performance of legal works,—as proof that not such works, but rather faith, is the condition of acceptance with God. This truth he has also confirmed by showing through the testimony of Scripture (a) that Abraham was justified by faith, and (b) that all the nations are to be partakers of the grace of God on the same terms with him. His next step is to prove from the Holy Scriptures:

3. THAT NO SINNER CAN BE JUSTIFIED AND BLESSED BY GOD ON THE GROUND OF HIS OBEDIENCE TO THE LAW. (10-12.)—Lightfoot's summary or paraphrase is excellent: "Having shown by positive proof that justification is of faith, he strengthens his position by the negative argument derived from the impossibility of maintaining its opposite, justification by law. This negative argument is twofold: First, it is impossible to fulfill the requirements of the law, and the non-fulfillment lays us under a curse (ver. 10); secondly, supposing the fulfillment possible, still the spirit of the law is antagonistic to faith, which is elsewhere spoken of as the source of life. (ver. 11, 12.)" Compare the analysis of Hackett before the notes on ver. 1.

10. For as many as are of the works of the law are under the (a) curse. This is introduced by 'for,' because it is meant to be a confirmation of the conclusion just stated, that men are justified through faith. The general premise admitted by all Christians was that men may be justified. The special premise here assumed is that this must be effected in one of two opposite ways, through faith or through obedience to law. Having produced evidence from the experience of the Galatian believers, and from the word of God, that men have been from of old until now justified through faith, he confirms his position that this is the way, and indeed the only

way, by showing from the same divine word that they cannot be justified by obedience to the law. Compare Rom. 4: 15. By those who 'are of works of law' are meant those "whose character is founded on works of law." Their spirit is the legal spirit, a spirit which is fostered by legal observances when these are looked upon as the ground of acceptance with God. The exact shade of thought intended here is probably "those who depend on them for justification." (Boise.) For it is written, Cursed is every one that continueth not in all things which are written in the book of the law, to do them. See Deut. 27 : 26. Quoted freely from the Septuagint which, in turn, is a free translation of the Hebrew. For the Hebrew reads: "Cursed be he that confirmeth not the words of this law to do them"; the Septuagint, "Cursed be every man that continueth not in all the words of this law to do them"; and Paul, as above, inserts the words, 'in the book of,' and substitutes 'the things written in' for 'the words of.' But these changes do not affect the sense of the passage. They merely serve to bring out more distinctly the meaning contained in the briefer original. The word 'cursed' signifies "condemned and suffering God's just displeasure." The effect of that condemnation was not, in the case of the chosen people, reserved altogether to a future state. It often took the form of temporal calamities. Yet under the clearer light of the Saviour's teaching we learn that it will eventuate in eternal ruin. The final clause, 'to do them,' describes the way in which one must 'confirm' or 'continue in' all the requirements of the law, in order to escape condemnation. Perfect obedience, obedience in all things, is demanded. Transgression in one point is sin. James refers to the same fact: "For whosoever shall keep the whole law, and yet stumble in one point, he is become guilty of all." (2 : 10.) Paul's statement, then, means that all who depend upon works of the law for justification are condemned; for every one who fails to obey that law perfectly is condemned, and every man has failed and will fail to obey it thus.

11 But that no man is justified by the law in the sight of God, it is evident: for, The just shall live by faith.

12 And the law is not of faith: but, The man that doeth them shall live in them.

11 law to do them. Now that no man is justified [1] by the law in the sight of God, is evident: for, The righteous shall live by faith; and the law is not of faith; but, He that doeth them shall live in them.

---

1 Gr. *in.*

Hence justification by legal works is impossible, and as many as rely upon them for it are under a curse. To make this doubly certain he presents the matter in another light, as follows:

11. **But (now) that no man is justified by the law in the sight of God, it is evident: for, The just (*righteous*) shall live by faith.** Compare Rom. 1:17; 3:21, seq.; Heb. 10:38. The cogency of this reasoning depends on the assumption that justification by legal works cannot blend with or be co-ordinate with justification by faith. The methods differ radically; one excludes the other. And this is the more evident after what is said in the preceding verse, which really shows that the only persons to be justified are sinners. 'By the law' might be rendered 'in the law,' that is, in its sphere and domain, where it determines the standing of every one. 'The righteous shall live by faith.' See Hab. 2:4. Another rendering which is adopted by many scholars, connects 'faith' with the adjective 'righteous' instead of the verb 'shall live,' thus: 'He, who is righteous by faith, shall live.' This rendering suits the argument of Paul better than the ordinary one, but it is not so natural a translation of the original text. For that appears to mean: 'The righteous man will live through his steadfast trust' (in God). "The word rendered 'faith'," says Cook, in the "Bible Commentary," "has the fundamental sense of steadfastness, hence trustworthiness, faithfulness in the discharge of all duties, especially of promises; as a personal quality, truth in deed and word, and in man's relation to God, firm belief and reliance on the divine promise, the special sense in this passage; whatever may betide others who "will not believe" (Hab. 1:5), the righteous who believes and trusts will live. That the word is properly rendered 'faith,' taken in the full, true sense of trustful faith, is clear from the usage of the word in the palmary text: "And he believed the Lord, and he counted it to him for righteousness." (Gen. 15:6.) That such reliance or faith is meant in our passage is evident; it is demanded by a clause in the preceding verse: "wait for it." (Hab. 2:3.)

And the law is not of faith. That is, according to the apostle, faith is not the working principle of the law, the idea from which it proceeds and upon which it depends for its efficacy. Compare Rom. 10:5. **But, the man that doeth (or, *hath done*) them shall live in them.** An abbreviated quotation of Lev. 18:5: "Ye shall keep my statutes, and my judgments, which if a man do, he shall live in them." Hence obedience is the condition of true life under the law. Doing, not believing, is the central idea of the legal system. He that has done what the law requires shall have life in and by the works which he has performed. By epitomizing the words of Leviticus so freely, Paul shows that he believed the Galatians to be familiar with this part of the Old Testament. It is possible that he had himself used it for a similar purpose when with them, and equally possible that it was frequently used by the Judaizing teachers who had come among them since his last visit. To infer from the apostle's free manner of citing the Old Testament in this instance that the Galatians were known by him to be well acquainted with the entire Old Testament would be going too far; yet a similar usage meets us in the Epistle to the Romans, and it is perfectly safe to conclude that he was in the habit of appealing to the Old Testament in his preaching, and that the churches founded by him, as well as those founded by the apostles of the circumcision, were taught to search the Scriptures to see 'whether these things were so.' (Acts 17:11.) A good example for all to follow! No part of the Bible has become antiquated and useless, and no class of men is excused from the direct examination of the sacred record. It was given to the people originally, and was adapted to their capacity. It is suited to them now, for their intelligence is not inferior to that of men in the apostolic age.

Having shown that all who rely upon legal

13 Christ hath redeemed us from the curse of the law, being made a curse for us; for it is written, Cursed is every one that hangeth on a tree:

14 That the blessing of Abraham might come on the Gentiles through Jesus Christ; that we might receive the promise of the Spirit through faith.

13 Christ redeemed us from the curse of the law, having become a curse for us: for it is written, Cursed is 14 every one that hangeth on a tree: that upon the Gentiles might come the blessing of Abraham in Christ Jesus; that we might receive the promise of the Spirit through faith.

works for justification before God are under a curse, the apostle now explains how it is—

4. THAT SOME THROUGH THE EXERCISE OF FAITH HAVE BEEN DELIVERED FROM THAT CURSE. (13, 14.)

13. Christ hath redeemed us from the curse of the law, being made (*having become*) a curse for us. The sense would be truly expressed if the last clause were translated 'by becoming a curse for us.' For the participle shows how the redemption was effected, rather than something which preceded that redemption. And the word 'redeemed' signifies, literally, 'bought out from,' in this case from the curse or condemnation of the violated law. It is most frequently applied to the act of ransoming one from slavery. The particular way in which 'Christ hath redeemed us,' by becoming a curse for us, is explained by the following quotation. And the sense in which he became a curse for us is explained in some measure by the apostle's language in 2 Cor. 5:21: "Him who knew no sin he made to be sin in our behalf, that we might become the righteousness of God in him." He suffered death, as though he were a sinner, in behalf of those who were sinners. He bore the punishment due to them for their sins. The noun 'curse' is more forcible than the adjective 'cursed.' Besides, in the Jewish ritual "the victim is regarded as bearing the sins of those for whom atonement is made. The curse is transferred from them to it. It becomes in a certain sense the impersonation of the sin and of the curse. This idea is very prominent in the scapegoat." (Lightfoot.) For it is written—or, 'because it has been written.' That is to say, in the Sacred Scriptures. When this formula is used in the New Testament it always refers to something which stands written in the Old Testament. So high was the character of that volume, so absolutely unique its position and authority, that it alone was suggested when anything was spoken of as written, unless some qualifying statement was added. Cursed is every one that hangeth on a tree. This expression is taken from the Septuagint of Deut. 21:23,

with an omission of the words 'by God,' thus: "For every one hanged upon a tree is cursed by God." The Hebrew of Deut. 21:22, 23, is thus translated in the Revised Version: "And if a man have committed a sin worthy of death, and he be put to death, and thou hang him on a tree; his body shall not remain all night upon the tree, but thou shalt bury him the same day: for he that is hanged is accursed by God." Hanging was a public exposure after death in the case of great criminals, which added to the ignominy and shame of their punishment. Jesus Christ, then, suffered death in a form prescribed for the worst criminals, and was treated after a manner which signified that the curse of God rested on him. His body was not allowed to remain upon the cross over night, but was treated as something accursed. The clause is a parenthesis, and the next verse is to be connected with the first part of this; namely, 'Christ redeemed us from the curse of the law by becoming a curse for us.'

14. That the blessing of Abraham might come on the Gentiles through (*in*) Jesus Christ. That blessing, as before shown, was obtained through faith, and not by obedience to the law—a thought which was now burnt into the minds of the Galatians. That we might receive the promise of the Spirit through faith. The 'we' is here comprehensive of all, whether Jews or Gentiles, who have true faith in Christ. For this blessing, the fulfillment of the promise of the Holy Spirit, or the promised Spirit, was bestowed on believing Gentiles as well as believing Jews, and it is scarcely natural to suppose that the apostle here thinks of Jews only, especially as he began his argument with the Galatians by appealing to the Spirit's work in them, when and after they believed. "The Holy Spirit is the divine power of that life in which the blessing promised to Abraham consists; he founds it, regulates its development, and pledges its completion; therefore he is called the Spirit of life. (Rom. 8:2.)" (Sieffert.) 'Through faith'—faith is the organ by which the Spirit is received. From these

15 Brethren, I speak after the manner of men; Though it be but a man's covenant, yet if it be confirmed, no man disannulleth, or addeth thereto.
16 Now to Abraham and his seed were the promises made. He saith not, And to seeds, as of many; but as of one, And to thy seed, which is Christ.

15 Brethren, I speak after the manner of men: Though it be but a man's covenant, yet when it hath been confirmed, no one maketh it void, or addeth 16 thereto. Now to Abraham were the promises spoken, and to his seed. He saith not, And to seeds, as of many; but as of one, And to thy seed, which is

verses (13, 14) it appears that Paul regarded the vicarious death of Christ as necessary, in order to the fulfillment of the promise to Abraham. Human salvation depends upon the death of the Redeemer as a propitiatory sacrifice, and has always depended on that death.

Paul next proceeds to show—

5. That the Promise to Abraham Cannot have been Annulled or Changed by the Law which was Given Long Afterward. (15-18.) Compare Rom. 4 : 13, 14, 16.

15. Brethren, I speak after the manner of men. Observe the cordial address, 'brethren.' The feelings of love and kindness are deep in the apostle's heart, and they now find expression. 'After the manner of men'—that is to say, 'I am about to use an illustration from man's way of dealing with man.' **Though it be but a man's covenant, yet if it be confirmed, no man disannulleth, or addeth thereto.** There seems to be no absolute necessity for the insertion of 'but' in the first clause, and therefore, as it represents no word in the original, it may be better to omit it, thus: 'A covenant which has been ratified, though a man's, yet no one sets aside or adds to it.' The word 'man's' is emphatic, in contrast with the word 'God's,' understood. That is, when a contract between different men is once ratified or confirmed, it cannot be changed by setting it aside altogether, or by adding new stipulations. It is fixed and sacred.

16. Now to Abraham and his seed were the promises made. See Revised Version and Gen. 13 : 15; 22 : 17, 18. It is the words 'and his seed' which Paul uses in the following exposition. His argument has been freely criticised as Rabbinical, and by Baur as "plainly arbitrary and incorrect." But it is our duty to hesitate long before charging the apostle with unsound interpretation or doctrine. Very likely his thought is deeper than we perceive, and worthy of admiration, rather than of contempt. Certainly he was correct in looking upon these promises as having more reference to the seed of Abraham than to Abraham himself. Let

his exposition then receive close attention, and just, if not generous, treatment!

He saith not, And to seeds, as of many; but as of one, And to thy seed, which is Christ. On this verse Dr. Hackett says: "The apostle does not refer here to any particular passage in the Old Testament which contains these words . . . ; but avails himself of this compendious mode of speaking as a convenient formula for summing up the entire teaching of the Scriptures on this subject. It will be noticed that the singular and the plural differ in this, that 'seed' (σπέρμα) denotes a unity of genus or class with a plurality of parts (as, for example, the wheat is one, though the kernels are many), and 'seeds' (σπέρματα) a plurality of classes, as wheat, barley, rye. Compare 'seed' (זֶרַע) in 1 Sam. 8 : 15. It is, therefore, as if Paul had said: "Search the Scriptures from Genesis to Malachi; the promises all run in one strain; they make no mention of a plurality of seeds, such as a natural and spiritual seed, at the same time; they speak of a single seed only, the believing race, those who are like Abraham in his faith (see Rom. 4 : 12), whether Jews or Gentiles; and as this restriction of the language to the one seed limits and exhausts the promises as to any share in the blessings of Abraham's justification, there are no promises of this nature for other seeds, such as Abraham's natural descendants, merely as such, or Jews by adoption, in virtue of their submission to Jewish rites." It may be observed: (1) That the promises made to Abraham were made also to his spiritual 'seed,' the collective noun denoting one body of posterity, not several bodies. Compare ver. 7, 9, 14, above. (2) That Christ was the glory of Abraham's seed, the One whose trust in God was absolute, and in whom pre-eminently all the nations were to be blessed. (3) That Christ is the unifying power in all true believers. In him they are 'one' person' (εἷς). See ver. 28. Indeed, it has been said that Paul was fully justified in regarding all the promises as made to Christ, because Christ was the principle of spiritual life in Abraham and in all who, like

17 And this I say, *that* the covenant, that was confirmed before of God in Christ, the law, which was four hundred and thirty years after, cannot disannul, that it should make the promise of none effect.

17 Christ. Now this I say; A covenant confirmed beforehand by God, the law, which came four hundred and thirty years after, doth not disannul, so as to

---

him, believe. To Christ, dwelling by his Spirit in the faithful of every age, were the promises really made. Compare the notes of Ellicott, Lightfoot, Cook, Beet, on this passage; also Balentine in "Bibliotheca Sacra," 1885, page 568, and on the other side of the question Bauer, Meyer, and others. The argument of the apostle is not without difficulty, but there is no ground for the charge that it is fallacious. Much rather should we suppose that it rests upon a deeper view of the unity of believers with Christ than is commonly entertained. To this fact Paul often refers in language of startling force.

17. Now this I say—in other words, 'This is my meaning, the principal thought which I have to express in connection with my remark concerning a man's covenant.' The conjunction ' now ' (δέ) is resumptive; for the apostle's argument had been interrupted momentarily by the explanation of 'his seed,' in ver. 16. **The covenant that was confirmed before of** (*by*) **God in Christ, the law, which was** (*came*) **four hundred and thirty years after, cannot disannul** (or, *annul*) **that it should make the promise of none effect** —that is, if human covenants once ratified are sacred and cannot be abrogated or essentially modified afterward, much less can the law, which was given long after the covenant had been established by God himself with Abraham, annul the promise contained in that covenant. Whatever else may have been the design of the law, it cannot have been intended to set aside, or to modify by new terms, the promise of justification through faith. "The gifts and the calling of God are without repentance." (Rom. 11 : 29.)

But though the bearing of this verse on Paul's argument is very clear, objection has been made to it as containing an erroneous chronological statement. For the words, ' which came four hundred and thirty years after,' are said to imply that the whole period, from the first giving of the promise to Abraham to the giving of the law, was only four hundred and thirty years; while Exod. 12 : 40, 41, where, and where only the same period is mentioned, shows that the sojourn of the Is-

raelites in Egypt was four hundred and thirty years. Compare the language of Stephen in Acts 7 : 6, and Hackett's note on the same. The sojourn in Egypt is there spoken of in round numbers as four hundred years. But, according to the best computation, two hundred and fifteen years elapsed between the time when the promise was first given and the time when Jacob and his sons went down into Egypt at the invitation of Joseph; so that the law came more than six hundred years after the promise. What shall be said of this discrepancy? This, in the first place, that Paul's reasoning is not affected in the slightest degree by the length of the period. The law was given long after the promise—whether four hundred and thirty years or six hundred and forty-five years, more or less, is of no consequence. It was enough for him to refer to the period in such terms as would bring it distinctly before the minds of his readers. He is not fixing points of chronology, but recalling a well-known period. Accordingly—

1. Paul may have followed the Septuagint, which contains an addition to the Hebrew text of Exod. 12 : 40, making it read, ' in the land of Egypt *and in the land of Canaan*,' and may have done this because the Greek version was sufficiently accurate for his purpose and was generally used by the Galatians. His object was not to teach them Biblical chronology, but to remind them of the fact that the law was given long after the promise, and could not be supposed to destroy or change the latter.

2. He may have followed the Hebrew text, making the *close*, instead of the *beginning* of the patriarchal age, the starting point in his reckoning; for the promise was repeated to Isaac and Jacob, and was, therefore, contemporaneous with the whole patriarchal period. With this would agree the plural, ' promises,' in ver. 16, if this plural relates to a repetition of essentially the same promise, which is certainly probable.

3. He may have followed the Septuagint Version, because it was correct in sense. In support of this view, which limits the actual sojourn of Israel in Egypt to two hundred

18 For if the inheritance *be* of the law, *it is* no more
of promise: but God gave *it* to Abraham by promise.
19 Wherefore then *serveth* the law? It was added

18 make the promise of none effect. For if the inheritance is of the law, it is no more of promise: but God
19 hath granted it to Abraham by promise. What then
is the law? It was added because of transgressions,

and fifteen years, appeal is made to Exod.
6 : 20 and Num. 26 : 59; for, according to
these passages, "Amram, grandson of Levi,
marries his father's sister, Jochebed." And,
as it appears probable by a comparison of
dates that Levi was born when Jacob was
about eighty-seven, Levi would have been
forty-three when he came into Egypt; there
he lives ninety-four years. (Exod. 6 : 16.) Assuming, then, that Jochebed was born in the
last year of Levi's life,—which is by no means
probable,—she must have been at least two
hundred and fifty-six years old when Moses
was born, if the sojourn in Egypt be four
hundred and thirty years." (Ellicott.) If
there are no missing links in the genealogy
of Exod. 6 : 20 and of Num. 26 : 59, the sojourn of the Israelites in Egypt could not
have lasted more than about two hundred and
fifteen years But the most obvious interpretation of a genealogical table is not always
trustworthy ; for unimportant names are frequently omitted from such a table. On the
whole, then, either the first or the second
explanation is preferable to the third ; but in
no case can the truthfulness of Paul's language be impeached.

18. For if the inheritance be (is) of the
law, it is no more of promise: but God
gave (hath given) it to Abraham by promise. 'For' makes this confirmatory of the
preceding words, 'so as to make the promise
of none effect.' It would be better, perhaps,
in this instance, to insert no article before the
word 'law': 'If the inheritance is of law, it
is no more of promise,' as it was before the
law was given. Yet the reference may be to
the law of Moses. 'Hath given.' The original word means hath freely given. Once
more, therefore, the apostle insists that true
heir-ship is a free gift. It cannot be earned
by obedience to the law. Justification is by
grace through faith.

The apostle now proceeds to point out—

6. THE OBJECT FOR WHICH THE LAW WAS
GIVEN ; NAMELY, TO AWAKEN IN MEN A
CONSCIOUSNESS OF SIN, AND THUS LEAD
THEM TO FAITH IN CHRIST. (3 : 19-24.)

"But if the law have no value as a means

of enabling us to establish a claim to the Divine favor, what end, the objector may ask,
was it designed to answer? (3:19.) In reply
to this question, the apostle explains the great
object of the law to be to prepare men for the
reception of the gospel by awakening them to
a consciousness of their sins and convincing
them of their need of the deliverance from
guilt and condemnation, which the redemption of Christ affords. (3:20-22.) We may
suppose that while Paul would describe this
as the office of law in general, and one, therefore, which it is adapted still to perform as a
means of bringing men to Christ, he means to
affirm it here more especially of the Mosaic
Economy, that great embodiment of the legal
principle which was established to prepare the
way for another and better system ; and then,
as to its outward forms, its rites and symbols,
was destined to come to an end. (3:23-25.)
Under this more perfect system which is realized in Christ, those who were only the natural
descendants of Abraham become by faith his
spiritual seed ; those who were servants, groan-
ing under the bondage of sin and the law,
become free. (3:26-29.) Those who were children in a state of minority and pupilage, are
advanced to the dignity of sons and heirs of
God, and receive the seal of their adoption as
such in the presence of the Spirit of God in
their hearts. (4:1-7.)" (Hackett.)

19. Wherefore then serveth the law?
—that is to say, *What is the object of the law?*
The same meaning would be gained by translating the question, '*Why then the law?*' If
men cannot be justified by means of it, what
good end does it serve, or why was it given?
The question which the apostle asks is one that
could hardly fail to arise in the minds of the
Galatians. Having been taught to accept the
Old Testament as a divine revelation, and the
law given by Moses as coming really from
God, it was impossible for them to believe
that it had no holy purpose to serve. And if
their teacher had now proved that no man
could be saved by obedience to it, they would
naturally insist upon his pointing out the
reason for its existence, the good end which
it was meant to accomplish. The apostle an-

because of transgressions, till the seed should come to whom the promise was made; *and it was ordained by angels in the hand of a mediator.*

20 Now a mediator is not a *mediator* of one, but God is one.

till the seed should come to whom the promise hath been made; *and it was ordained through angels by* 20 the hand of a mediator. Now a mediator is not a

swers: **It was added because of** (*the*) **transgressions.** The word translated 'because of' signifies, primarily, *for the sake of*, and it is best to retain that meaning here. Thayer's "Lexicon" explains the phrase "for the sake of transgressions" as meaning, "*to create transgressions*—that is, that sins might take on the character of transgressions, and thereby the consciousness of sin be intensified and the desire for redemption aroused." This interpretation is favored by the language of Paul in Rom. 5 : 20; 7 : 7-9, and by his discussion below. See ver. 22 and 24. It is the office of the law to awaken in men the consciousness of sin, in order that they may feel the need of a Saviour; for such is the nature of sinful men, as even heathen writers have confessed, that they are provoked by just restraint, and are sure to covet what is forbidden. Hence, conscious transgression is increased by a clear revelation of the law which it breaks, and the soul is made, at the same time, distinctly aware of its perverse self-will and inclination to wrong doing. It is, then, perfectly plain that actual transgression is often occasioned by law; and therefore the *proximate* purpose of law may be to multiply transgressions, though, in case of the divine law, its *ultimate* purpose is certainly to prepare the way for salvation through Christ. This is plainly asserted by the apostle in the sequel. **Till the seed should come to whom the promise was** (*hath been*) **made** (literally, *given*). According to ver. 16, 'the seed' must be Christ; and it is implied that the functions of the law were to become far less important after his coming. Indeed, the ritual parts of it were to be annulled and the moral parts assigned to their true place in the New Economy. Hence, all that was strictly distinctive in the law of Moses was to pass away. **And it was ordained by** (*through*) **angels in** (or, *by*) **the hand of a mediator.** The law was thus given. *Being ordained*, or, *having been ordained*, would be a literal version of the Greek, but less readable English than the one adopted by the Revisers. "By the hand of a mediator"; namely,

Moses, who received the law and made it known to the people. Though nothing is said in the book of Exodus concerning the ministration of angels at the giving of the law, their presence is referred to in Deut. 33 : 2, and their service in Acts 7 : 53 and Heb. 2 : 2. But it is useless to conjecture what precisely their service was. This only is implied by the argument here, as well as by the course of thought in Heb. 2 : 2, that the ministry of angels must be supposed to have diminished, rather than to have increased the intrinsic grandeur of the occasion and the importance of the law. A direct communication from God himself would have served to enhance the dignity and sacredness of that which was communicated. This will become more evident from our study of the next verse.

20. Now a mediator is not (*a mediator*) **of one; but God is one.** This language is confessedly dark. A great truth is hinted, rather than fully expressed. 'A mediator' (for the definite article in the Greek here marks the noun as generic), it is said in the first clause, does not belong to one; and **this** implies that he belongs to two, and that a covenant established between two, through the service of a mediator, must, from the nature of the case, depend for its fulfillment upon both. Thus was it, the apostle suggests, in the giving of the law through Moses. The blessing of it was conditioned upon its being honored by the people as well as by God. 'But God is one,' and in giving the promise he acted without a mediator, and made the fulfillment of his promise independent of human works. Says Sieffert: "The thought of ver. 20 in its historical application is the following: The law is inferior to the promise, because the mediator of it does not belong to God alone, but to him and the people of Israel at the same time, and this can only mean what was intimated in ver. 15-18, that the law, as a covenant relation, mediately established between God and the people, and depending for its validity upon the conduct of the people, can only represent the conditioned will of God, but cannot, as the promise given

21 *Is the law then against the promises of God?* God forbid: for if there had been a law given which could have given life, verily righteousness should have been by the law.

22 But the Scripture hath concluded all under sin, that the promise by faith of Jesus Christ might be given to them that believe.

23 But before faith came, we were kept under the law, shut up unto the faith which should afterwards be revealed.

21 *mediator* of one; but God is one. Is the law then against the promises of God? God forbid: for if there had been a law given which could make alive, verily righteousness would have been of the law.

22 Howbeit the scripture shut up all things under sin, that the promise by faith in Jesus Christ might be given to them that believe.

23 But before faith came, we were kept in ward under the law, shut up unto the faith which should

---

directly by himself, be an adequate expression of his absolute will, of his eternally valid purpose of salvation." [1]

21. Is the law then against the promises of God? God forbid! (*Let it not be!*) The connection between this verse and the preceding may be thus stated: "Having shown that the law is inferior to the promises, must we go a step further and conclude that it works against them, that it does anything to prevent their fulfillment or to render them less necessary to human salvation? Let such a thought never enter the mind! It is incredible. For, in the *first* place, it does not supersede the promise and render its fulfillment useless, for it cannot give spiritual life, justification, peace with God. (ver. 21.) And, in the *second* place, it prepares men for the grace which was promised through Christ by awakening in their hearts a sense of sin, and leading them to the Saviour. **For if there had been a law given which could have given life** (*make alive*), **verily righteousness should** (*would*) **have been of the law.** In this way, and in this alone, could the law work against the fulfillment of the promises. But, as before proved, it has no power to deliver men from sin and death. Its purpose is far humbler, though exceedingly important; and this purposed work of the law the apostle at once proceeds to explain.

22. But the Scripture hath concluded (*shut up*) **all** (*things*) **under sin, that the promise by faith of** (*in*) **Jesus Christ might be given to them that believe.** By 'the Scripture' must be meant the Old Testament,

and especially the law which it reveals, a law which shows every man to be a transgressor, having the guilt of sin resting upon him. The neuter, rendered 'all things,' is evidently used for the sake of emphasis in place of "all men." The object of God in giving the law was to bring men to a clearer and more pungent consciousness of sin, by making it take the form of definite transgressions. In other words, it was to make them understand their real inner life, their alienation from himself, and their need of his grace. In the last clause, 'the promise' is equivalent to *the fulfillment of the promise,* and 'by faith in Jesus Christ,' to *on condition of faith in Jesus Christ;* while the special importance of faith is shown by the double reference to it in the words, 'by faith in Jesus Christ,' and in the final expression, 'to them that believe.' Looking at salvation from the human side, it depends not upon works of obedience to the law, but upon faith in Jesus Christ, the Saviour of lost men. Even the law itself was intended to compel men to distrust the possibility of justification before God on the ground of obedience, and to trust alone in the mercy of God through the sacrifice of Jesus Christ. Thus the law is not 'against the promises,' but subservient to them.

23. But before faith (or, better, *the faith*) **came, we were kept** (*kept in ward*) **under the law, shut up unto the faith which should afterwards be revealed.** 'The faith' here means the system of doctrine of which faith is a distinguishing feature—the faith system. Compare Jude 3: "I was con-

---

[1] More than three hundred different explanations of the thought intended by this verse are said to have been given. The statement seems incredible, but human ingenuity is boundless. In the last edition of Meyer's "Commentary," Sieffert reduces 'the weightiest modern explanations' to three classes: 1. Those which find in the first half of the verse a tacit reference to the Mosaic Law, and a proof of its inferiority to the promise in the fact that a Mediator naturally implies *two* parties. 2. Those which find a tacit reference to the Mosaic Law in the first clause, with a proof of its inferiority to the promise in the fact that a mediator appertains, not to one, but to *many.* Thus Moses acted for the whole people. 3. Those which are too capricious and diverse to be brought under any one point of view.

Under each of these heads several expositors are named, and the special features of their interpretations criticised. Sieffert's explanation belongs to the first class.

24 Wherefore the law was our schoolmaster *to bring us unto Christ, that we might be justified by faith.*
25 But after that faith is come, we are no longer under a schoolmaster.
26 For ye are all the children of God by faith in Christ Jesus.

24 afterwards be revealed. So that the law is become our tutor *to bring us* unto Christ, that we might be
25 justified by faith. But now that faith is come, we
26 are no longer under a tutor. For ye are all sons of

strained to write unto you exhorting you to contend earnestly for the faith which was delivered once for all to the saints," where 'the faith' cannot easily be understood of subjective trust or belief: it must rather signify the Christian truth delivered to men and received by faith. For a believing spirit was not given once for all to the saints; it was the gospel to be believed which was thus given. So here 'the faith which should afterwards be revealed' cannot be subjective faith, but must be the gospel. Compare Acts 6 : 7; Jude 3. The pronoun 'we' appears to represent the Jewish Christians who, before the gospel came, proclaiming the way of life through faith in Christ, were guarded under the law, lest they might escape from its control. 'Shut up unto the faith about to be revealed.' In this clause, 'the faith' evidently means what is believed by Christians, not "the form in which the truth is subjectively appropriated" (Weiss, as quoted by Thayer)—that is, in brief, the gospel itself. Says Lightfoot: "The use of . . . faith in these verses (22, 23, 25) links together its extreme senses, passing from the one to the other: 1. Faith, the subjective state of the Christian; 2. *The* faith, the gospel, the objective teaching, the system of which 'faith' is the leading feature."

24. Wherefore the law was (*hath been*) **our schoolmaster** (*tutor*) **to bring us unto Christ, that we might be justified by faith.** The strict supervision and moral training of the law were a preparation for the freedom under Christ. Its office was similar to that of a pedagogue, or tutor, who has the care and control of children, watching them, restraining them, and often subjecting them to rigid discipline. "Among the Greek and Latin writers the idea of guardianship, and also of *strictness* and *severity*, is distinctly prominent." (Ellicott.) 'Unto Christ,' or for Christ, the preposition marking Christ as the object or end for which the law was a tutor. The law accomplished its pedagogic work by awakening a sense of sin, and thus preparing those under it to welcome the redemption purchased by Christ.

25. But after that faith, etc. (or, *now that the faith has come*) **we are no longer under a tutor.** If we understand 'the faith' to be, as in ver. 23, the message of faith, or the gospel, the coming of the gospel is here said by Paul to have changed the religious condition of Jewish believers, so that they were no longer under tutelage, but in a state of freedom. "Now, when faith is come, the schoolmaster, with his heavy and grievous office, is constrained to give place. . . . The law terrifieth and tormenteth us no more. . . . For Christ, taking upon him our flesh, came once into the world: he abolished the law with all its effects, and delivered from eternal death all those who receive his benefit by faith. If, therefore, ye look unto Christ, and that which he hath done, there is now no law. . . . And, since the law is gone, we are not kept under the tyranny thereof any more; but we live in joy and safety under Christ, who now sweetly reigneth in us by his Spirit." (Luther.) This, however, according to Luther, is the ideal view. There is another side to the Christian life in its present imperfect state. "According to the spirit, we serve with Paul, the 'law of God: but according to the flesh the law of sin.' . . . As long as we live in the flesh, which is not without sin, the law oftentimes returneth and doeth his office, in one more, and in another less, as their faith is strong or weak, and yet not to their destruction, but to their salvation. For this is the exercise of the law in the saints—namely, the continual mortification of the flesh, of reason, and of our own strength, and the daily renewing of our inward man."

Having thus explained the change in the religious condition of those Jews who had accepted the grace of God in Christ Jesus—

Tᴴᴱ Aᴘᴏsᴛʟᴇ ᴛᴜʀɴs ᴛᴏ ᴛʜᴇ Gᴀʟᴀᴛɪᴀɴs ᴀɴᴅ Dᴇsᴄʀɪʙᴇs ᴛʜᴇɪʀ Rᴇʟᴀᴛɪᴏɴ ᴛᴏ Gᴏᴅ ᴛʜʀᴏᴜɢʜ Fᴀɪᴛʜ.

26. For ye are all the children (*sons*) **of God, through faith in Christ Jesus**—literally, 'through *the* faith in Christ Jesus,' the faith which has been so often referred to in this discussion, and which has in Jesus Christ

D

27 For as many of you as have been baptized into Christ have put on Christ.

28 There is neither Jew nor Greek, there is neither bond nor free, there is neither male nor female: for ye are all one in Christ Jesus.

29 And if ye be Christ's, then are ye Abraham's seed, and heirs according to the promise.

27 God, through faith, in Christ Jesus. For as many of you as were baptized into Christ did put on

28 Christ. There can be neither Jew nor Greek, there can be neither bond nor free, there can be no male and female: for ye all are one *man* in Christ Jesus.

29 And if ye are Christ's, then are ye Abraham's seed, heirs according to promise.

its object and resting place. "He saith not, ye are the children of God because ye are circumcised, because ye have heard the law and have done the works thereof (as the Jews do imagine and the false apostles teach), but by faith in Jesus Christ. . . . What tongue, either of men or angels, can sufficiently extol and magnify the great mercy of God toward us, that we, who are miserable sinners, and by nature the children of wrath, should be called to his grace and glory, to be made the children and heirs of God, fellow-heirs with the Son of God, and lords over heaven and earth, and that by means of our faith only which is in Christ Jesus." (Luther.)

27. For as many of you as have been (*were*) **baptized into Christ have** (*did*) **put on Christ.** 'For' shows that this verse was written to confirm the preceding statement, to show that all believers in Christ, the Son of God, are so united with him as to be, in consequence of that union, also themselves sons of God. To express this, baptism must have represented the beginning of true faith in the soul. And the words, 'did put on Christ,' describe the act of baptism as their own act. They do not agree with the idea that baptism was intended to produce faith in any one who did not wish to be a servant of Christ, or to implant the germ of it in infants. All who were baptized did by that act avowedly put on Christ, did ritually and solemnly and publicly confess their having entered upon a new spiritual life of faith in the Son of God. Ellicott explains 'into Christ' as meaning, in this place, "into communion with him, and incorporation in his mystical body." He also says that "from the instances which Wettstein has collected on Rom. 13, 14, it would appear that 'to put on one' is a strong expression,

denoting the complete assumption of the nature, etc., of another." See Col. 3 : 9, 10.

28. There is (*can be*) **neither Jew nor Greek, there is** (*can be*) **neither bond nor free, there is** (*can be*) **neither male nor female: for ye all are one** (*man*) **in Christ Jesus.** See Revised Version. Lightfoot's paraphrase is excellent: "In Christ ye are all sons, all free. Every barrier is swept away. No special claims, no special liabilities exist in him; none *can* exist. The conventional distinctions of religious caste or of social rank, even the natural distinction of sex, are banished hence. One heart beats in all: one mind guides all: one life is lived by all: ye are all *one man*, for ye are members of Christ." The unity here affirmed relates to spiritual life and standing before God. It is, therefore, perfectly consistent with diversity of offices, duties, gifts—whether in the church or in the world. See the apostle's discussion in 1 Corinthians chapters 12 and 14. **There is**—or, *can be* (ἔνι). For the origin and meaning of the Greek word, see Thayer's "New Testament Lexicon," *sub voce;* Winer's "New Testament Grammar," page 80; and Ellicott, Lightfoot, and others on this passage. Compare Col. 3 : 11 and James 1 : 17, where the same word occurs. Thayer defines it, "*is in, is among, is present, has place*" for the New Testament; but says that in profane authors it often signifies "*can be, is possible, is lawful.*" Lightfoot explains its meaning here as "*there is no room for, place for.*"

29. And if ye be Christ's, then are ye Abraham's seed, and heirs according to the promise—that is, if you belong to the person of Christ, then, being one with him, the Seed to whom the promise was given, are ye Abraham's seed, heirs according to promise.

CHAPTER IV.

NOW I say, *That* the heir, as long as he is a child, differeth nothing from a servant, though he be lord of all;

2 But is under tutors and governors until the time appointed of the father.

3 Even so we, when we were children, were in bondage under the elements of the world:

1 But I say that so long as the heir is a child, he differeth nothing from a bondservant, though he is

2 lord of all; but is under guardians and stewards

3 until the term appointed of the father. So we also, when we were children, were held in bondage under

Ch. 1: The Apostle Describes the Relation of Christians to God as that of Sons and Heirs, Instead of Minors or Bondservants. (1-7.)--Dr. Hackett, as we have seen (3 : 18), understands these verses to teach that "those who were children in a state of minority and pupilage, are advanced to the dignity of sons and heirs of God, and receive the seal of their adoption as such in the presence of the Spirit of God in their hearts."

1. Now I say, That the heir, as long as he is a child, differeth nothing from a servant, though he be lord of all. Compare the Revised Version, which is more exact. The apostle now explains his conclusion that "if we are Christ's, then are we . . . heirs according to promise." (3 : 29.) The word translated 'child' is often applied to one who is but an infant, not having learned to speak; but it is also applied to one who is older, and here to one who has not reached his majority, so as to be able to speak for himself in business affairs. The English word 'infant' has by derivation the same primary sense, and in common use it signifies a babe, but in legal documents it often signifies a minor. 'Differeth nothing,' or in no respect, 'from a bondservant'—that is, his legal status is substantially that of a slave. He is subject to those who are placed over him by his father. This is assumed to be customary by the language of the verse, and there is no reason to call in question the correctness of this assumption. Doubtless there were points of difference between the ordinary treatment of minors and the ordinary treatment of slaves, but both were under the legal control of others. 'Though he be lord of all.' By nature and in his own right he is lord, while his present condition is like that of a servant.

2. But is under tutors and governors (better, *overseers and stewards*) **until the time** (Revised Version, *term*) **appointed of the father.** The distinction between 'overseers' and 'stewards' (ἐπιτρόπους καὶ οἰκονόμους) ap-

pears to be this—that the duties of the latter were commonly restricted to the care of the household, while the duties of the former were not thus restricted, but might include the care and training of children. 'Until the time appointed by the father.' The Greek (τῆς προθεσμίας) means *the before-appointed* day or hour, the word day (ἡμέρα), or hour (ὥρα) being understood. Yet the expression 'the term appointed' is sufficiently accurate, because the day or hour fixed was the terminus of a period. It is said that among the Hebrews, Greeks, and Romans, the age at which children ceased to be minors was fixed by law or custom, so that a father had nothing to do with that matter in making his last will and testament. He could select the guardians for his children, but could not appoint the day when the children should become of age. Some interpreters have supposed that a different custom prevailed in Galatia, "but this view," says Lightfoot, "seems to rest on a mistaken interpretation of a passage of Gaius —I, § 55." But is there any need of supposing that Paul has in mind the case of an heir whose father is dead? While both were living the father had supreme authority over the son, and often committed the son to the care of overseers, and the management of his estate to stewards. See Matt. 21 : 38; Luke 16 : 31. It is better, then, to assume that the apostle had in view the condition of children whose father was still alive.

3. Even so we, when we were children, were in bondage under the elements (*rudiments*) **of the world.** Does the 'we' refer to all Christians, whether Jews or Gentiles by birth, or to Jewish Christians alone? Lightfoot, Beet, Boise, and Sieffert hold that it means all Christians, especially in view of the following context, but Ellicott thinks that the primary reference is to converted Jews, as the previous context suggests, while there is a secondary reference to converted Gentiles, as the following verses show. Certainty on this

4 But when the fulness of the time was come, God sent forth his Son, made of a woman, made under the law,

5 To redeem them that were under the law, that we might receive the adoption of sons.

4 the [1] rudiments of the world: but when the fulness of the time came, God sent forth his Son, born of a woman, born under the law, that he might redeem them that were under the law, that we might re-

2 Or, elements.

point is beyond our reach, but we incline to the opinion that Paul has in mind Christians without regard to nationality. This is favored by the last part of the verse, 'were held in bondage under the rudiments of the world.' What, then, is meant by 'the rudiments of the world' (τὰ στοιχεῖα τοῦ κόσμου)? The word translated rudiments signifies: (1) The elements of speech, the letters of the alphabet. (2) The elements, or a, b, c, of any art, science, discipline, or religion. See Heb. 5: 12, 13; Gal. 4: 9; Col. 2: 8, 20. (3) The elements of the physical universe. (2 Peter 3: 10, 12.) (4) The heavenly bodies. The word is used in only the second and third senses by New Testament writers. Here it must denote the crude, elementary ideas of religion which were known to the heathen as well as to the Jews, which were in fact the possession of the world of mankind, and which were embodied in ritual acts testifying of sin, but bringing no peace to conscience. The burdensome rites of Judaism, as they were taught and practiced by many in Paul's day, were just as powerless before God as were the superstitious forms of idolatry. Neither of them brought the freedom of sonship to God. Both of them kept the souls of their devotees in bondage and fear. And this was the condition of all who clung to mere legalism before the advent of Christ.

4. But when the fulness of the time was come (or, *came*). This language answers to 'the time appointed by the father' in ver. 2, and according to Meyer signifies "the moment through which the period of time which was to pass before the Saviour came was made full." But why so long a period was fixed by the wisdom of God before the advent of his Son, no one has been able to explain. Some have thought it was precisely adapted to the moral or religious preparation which the world, and especially the chosen people, needed for the coming of Christ. Others have thought that it was fixed at the hour "when human nature, having gone through every form of wickedness, was in need of healing." Theophylact says that Christ came "in the hour of supremest need"; and Chrysostom, that when "men were specially near destruction, then they were saved." No reverent Christian can doubt that he came at the best moment possible. But the apostle simply affirms that when the pre-Messianic period was completed, **God sent forth his Son, made** (*born*) **of a woman, made** (*born*) **under the law.** 'Forth'—that is, away from his presence, or, more accurately, from 'the glory which he had with the Father before the world was.' (John 17: 5; compare 1: 1 and 1 John 1: 2.) The apostle starts with the incarnation, though his words may embrace Christ's appearance among men. Many interpreters look upon this passage as one of a few in the New Testament which teach the proper Sonship of the Word (λόγος) to the Father before the incarnation. This may have been in the apostle's mind, but I do not see that it *must* have been. Could he not have said, "God sent forth Jesus Christ, born of a woman, born under the law," though he did not intend to say that Jesus Christ as such was pre-existent? And if so, could he not write, 'God sent forth his Son, born of a woman, born under the law,' though he did not intend to say that the Word was, strictly speaking, Son before the incarnation? Compare his language in Phil. 2: 6, where the pronoun "who," in the clause "who being in the form of God," represents "Jesus Christ," the only possible antecedent. As Jesus Christ, by virtue of his higher nature, existed, before his humiliation, in the form of God, so God's Son, the same Jesus Christ, by virtue of his higher nature, was sent forth from glory, etc.

There is surely nothing absurd in this interpretation. The clauses, 'born of a woman, born under the law,' describe certain great features of the incarnation. The former calls attention to his genuine humanity. He was a veritable man. His human nature was derived from the common stock. He partook with his brethren of flesh and blood. But he was also a Jew, 'born under the law' and subject to all its requirements.

5. To redeem (*that he might redeem*)

6 And because ye are sons, God hath sent forth the Spirit of his Son into your hearts, crying, Abba, Father.
7 Wherefore thou art no more a servant, but a son: and if a son, then an heir of God through Christ.

6 ceive the adoption of sons. And because ye are sons, God sent forth the Spirit of his Son into our 7 hearts, crying, Abba, Father. So that thou art no longer a bondservant, but a son; and if a son, then an heir through God.

them that were under the law, that we might receive the adoption of sons. 'Them that were under the law'—literally, 'those under law,' meaning, doubtless, the law of Moses. Yet the Jewish law was not different in principle from any other revelation of God's law. All men are naturally under law, and by it are condemned as transgressors, unless they have been ransomed by the blood of Christ. For all are guilty of doing what they knew to be wrong, and when their consciences are awake, if at no other time, they see themselves to be under condemnation. Hence, their frantic efforts to appease imaginary gods, and the hopelessness with which they look into the future. Seeing no prospect of deliverance from the bondage and curse of the law, as it is revealed to them, they long for annihilation, or, at least, for the rest of existence without feeling. In the last clause, 'that we might receive the adoption of sons,' the 'we' embraces all Christians, whether Jews or Gentiles. And adoption is the divine act of assigning to believers in Christ the position and privileges of sons. "It is a favorite thought with the apostle that the Christian is the adopted son of God. He is not merely a proselyte brought from another nation to share the privileges of the Jewish people; he is made a member of the family of Christ. The custom of adoption was familiar both to the Greek and the Roman law, and is used by the apostle, who was the Roman citizen of a Greek city, like some other legal notions (Rom. 7 : 1; Gal. 3 : 15; 4 : 1) to express the relations of God and man." (Jowett.) Whether the preposition in the Greek word for 'that we might receive' (ἀπολάβωμεν) signifies that the adoption of sons was looked upon by Paul as a good received in fulfillment of a promise, or as a good received back again after being lost, or merely as a good received from another, cannot easily be decided; but the last explanation is open to fewer objections than either of the preceding.

For the adoption of sons is not here spoken of as promised, and it includes far more than Adam had before the fall. See Ellicott and Meyer, and compare the use of the same verb in Luke 16 : 25.[1]

6. And because ye are sons, God hath sent forth the Spirit of his Son into your hearts, crying, Abba, Father. Union with Christ, sonship to God, and inworking of the Holy Spirit are inseparable blessings, and the apostle here points out their logical order and relation. The Galatians had been endued with the Holy Spirit (3 : 2, seq.), because they were sons of God by adoption. It is this Spirit that cries from their hearts through their lips, 'Abba, Father.' In other words, it is this Spirit who gives them filial love and confidence, so that they call upon God as their Father in heaven. Observe, however, that the language of Paul recognizes the Holy Spirit as pertaining to 'his Son,' Jesus Christ. Compare John 15 : 26; 16 : 7; Rom. 8 : 9; Phil. 1 : 19; Acts 17 : 7; 1 Peter 1 : 10, 11; 2 Cor. 3 : 17, 18. Hence the filioque, the 'proceeding' of the Holy Spirit from the Son, as well as from the Father, is manifestly the teaching of the divine word. But the procession spoken of or implied in these passages cannot properly be understood of an eternal process within the Trinity, but must be referred to the action of the Spirit in renewing and sanctifying men, or in revealing to them religious truth.

7. Wherefore (or, so that) thou art no more (longer) a servant, but a son; and if a son, then (or, also) an heir of (through) God. By changing the address from 'ye' to 'thou,' Paul renders his words more personal and impressive. For 'thou' means every separate Christian among the Galatians. In the last clause of ver. 5 it is 'we'; in ver. 6 it is 'ye'; and now in ver. 7 it is 'thou.' Notice the reiteration and expansion of the same thought in Rom. 8 : 14-17: "For as many as

[1] The compound verb ἀπολαμβάνειν occurs in the following passages: Luke 15 : 27; 16 : 25; 18 : 30; 23 : 41; Rom. 1 : 27; Col. 3 : 24; 2 John 8. And it seems to me that the word signifies to receive from some person or place, without any implication in itself that what is received is pay or punishment, or had been promised or possessed before. These things depend on the context, not on the verb.

8 Howbeit then, when ye knew not God, ye did service unto them which by nature are no gods.
9 But now, after that ye have known God, or rather are known of God, how turn ye again to the weak and beggarly elements, whereunto ye desire again to be in bondage?

8 Howbeit at that time, not knowing God, ye were in bondage to them that by nature are no gods: but now that ye have come to know God, or rather to be known of God, how turn ye back again to the weak and beggarly ¹ rudiments, whereunto ye desire to

---

1 Or, *elements.*

---

are led by the Spirit of God, they are the sons of God. For ye received not the spirit of bondage again to fear; but ye have received the Spirit of adoption, whereby we cry, Abba, Father. The Spirit itself beareth witness with our spirit, that we are children of God: and if children, then heirs; heirs of God and joint-heirs with Christ; if so be that we suffer with him, that we may be also glorified together (*with him*)." What more is it possible for Christians to have?

But why does the apostle say (for this is the correct reading), 'an heir *through* God,' when we might rather expect him to say 'an heir of God'? Probably because he was thinking at this moment of God as the one by whom every heir to himself, save Christ, had been adopted, because he was thinking more of the privilege and glory of being made a son by God's own gracious act than of the blessedness that would result from the relation thus established. To think of either is enough to break the heart with joy.

THE FOLLY OF THE GALATIANS IN RE-TURNING TO THE BONDAGE OF LEGALISM. (8–11.)—"In view of this superiority of the Christian Dispensation to the Jewish, Paul then remonstrates with the Galatians on their folly and ingratitude in turning back to the beggarly elements of the past. (4:8-11.) He adds his most earnest entreaty that they would return and trust again with him in Christ; he strengthens this appeal by a touching allusion to their former affection for him, and distinctly apprises them that in becoming alienated from him they had been made the dupes of artful men, whose pretended zeal for the law origi-nated in a selfish regard for their own ease and reputation. (4:12-20.)" (Hackett.)

8. Howbeit then, when ye knew not God, ye did service unto them which by nature are no gods. See the Revised Version. 'Did service' should be rendered, 'did bondservice,' or 'were in bondage,' for this is the proper meaning of the word, and besides it carries forward the representation of bond-age emphasized in the preceding context. It properly characterizes the service. From this verse it may be inferred that nearly all the Galatian Christians had been idolaters. In-deed, the whole Epistle makes upon one the impression that its readers were converts from heathenism. They had been in bondage to those that by nature were not gods, though they were called gods and were served with fear. The word 'howbeit' is a somewhat vague word, used in this place to avoid the employ-ment of 'but' in two successive clauses. The original (ἀλλὰ) is, however, best represented by the ordinary equivalent 'but.'

9. But now, after that ye have known God, or rather are known of God. The word translated 'have known' differs from that translated 'knew' in ver. 8, and may be rendered, 'have come to know' or 'have rec-ognized.' See Revised Version.¹

'Or rather are known of God'—that is, by God. This clause appears to have been in-serted by the apostle, lest perchance the Gala-tians might assign undue importance to their recognition and knowledge of God, while God's recognition of them was infinitely more important, as well as more perfect. Compare 1 Cor. 8:2 and 13:12. Or if the idea of 'ap-probation' is involved in the word as here used, how instantly does God's knowledge of them fill the mind and expel every thought of their knowledge of him! The latter is the more probable explanation. How turn ye again to the weak and beggarly elements,

---

¹ The note of Lightfoot on the two words is instruct-ive. "Thus γινώσκειν will be used in preference to εἰδέναι: 1. Where there is reference to some earlier state of ignorance, or to some prior facts on which the knowledge is based. 2. Where the ideas of 'thorough-ness, familiarity,' or of 'approbation,' are involved:

these ideas arising out of the stress which γινώσκειν lays on the *process* of reception. Both words occur very frequently in the First Epistle of St. John, and a com-parison of the passages where they are used brings out this distinction of meaning clearly."

10 Ye observe days, and months, and times, and years.

11 I am afraid of you, lest I have bestowed upon you labour in vain.

12 Brethren, I beseech you, be as I am; for I am as ye are: ye have not injured me at all.

10 be in bondage over again? Ye observe days, and months, and seasons, and years. I am afraid of you, lest by any means I have bestowed labour upon you in vain.

12 I beseech you, brethren, become as I am, for I also

whereunto ye desire again to be in bondage? The Revised Version reads 'back again,' instead of 'again,' in the first clause of this question. The apostle here speaks as if the process were already begun, as if they were now perpetrating the folly described by him. 'The elements' of religion possessed by the Galatians before their conversion are characterized as 'weak,' because they had no power to deliver men from condemnation; and 'beggarly' or 'poor,' because they utterly failed to enrich the soul with any real good. And in neither of these respects would the legal observances of Judaism prove to be any better than those of paganism. The Greek words employed (πάλιν ἄνωθεν) are inadequately rendered by 'again' in the Common Version. 'Over again' in the Revised Version is an improvement, especially if Lightfoot is correct in pronouncing them "a strong expression to describe the completeness of their *relapse*." But it is better to regard the second word (ἄνωθεν) as signifying 'afresh' or 'anew,' and the two words as meaning that their proposed form of legal religion was a fresh start on an old way, a resumption *de novo* of a religious life which they had known and relinquished. Compare the use of the second word (ἄνωθεν) in John 3 : 3.

10. Ye observe days, and months, and times (*seasons*), and years. This may be read as a question: "Days do ye scrupulously observe and months, and seasons, and years?" But with that change the meaning would remain essentially the same. The Galatians seem to have begun to keep some of the Jewish sacred times, perhaps the Jewish Sabbath, thus committing themselves in principle to the keeping of all the rest. The word 'days' probably refers to the weekly sabbaths and other set days observed by the Jews. See Col. 3 : 16 and Rom. 14 : 5, seq. There is no ground for believing that Paul embraced the Lord's Day in this category. The word 'months' is commonly supposed to signify in this place *new moons*—that is, the first day of every month. See Num. 10 : 10; 28 : 11; Isa. 1 : 13; Hosea 2 : 11; 1 Chron. 23 : 31; Ps. 81 : 3.

'Seasons' must mean the periods allotted to the annual festivals, such as the Passover, the Pentecost, the Feast of the Ingathering, etc.; and 'years,' the seventh sabbatic year, together with the fiftieth or Jubilee. Meyer and Sieffert maintain the opinion that 'months' does not signify new moons, but rather periods of a full month, and that certain months of every year were esteemed specially sacred. This, however, is less probable than the view given above. For if any months were specially sacred, it must have been because of the religious festivals observed in them, and these festivals are doubtless meant by the word 'seasons.' To suppose them twice mentioned is unnatural. Dr. Boise takes the enumeration to be of a general nature, thus: "Days—years: a general expression (which we should not attempt to define too particularly) with reference to the Jewish observance of times and seasons."

11. I am afraid of you, lest I have bestowed upon you labour in vain. Revised Version: *lest by any means*. This fear reveals the danger to which they were exposed and the deep interest which the apostle felt in their welfare. They were on the point of turning away from the true and full gospel which they had received, to a religion of works that would prove their ruin. Should they really do what they were solicited to do, it would be a renunciation of confidence in Christ as their Saviour, and a virtual rejection of the gospel.

PERSONAL APPEAL TO THE GALATIANS. (12-20.) See Hackett's analysis before ver. 8, seq.

12. Brethren, I beseech you, be as I am; for I am as ye are. Says Dr. Hackett: "A more correct translation . . . would be: 'Become as I am, for I also have become as ye are, brethren, I beseech you.' The passage has been treated as needlessly obscure. We have the key which unlocks the meaning in 1 Cor. 9 : 20, 21. "Unto the Jews," Paul says there, "I became as a Jew, that I might gain the Jews; . . . to them that are without law (I became) as without law, that I might gain them that are without law"

13 Ye know how through infirmity of the flesh I preached the gospel unto you at the first.

13 *am become* as ye are. Ye did me no wrong; but ye know that because of an infirmity of the flesh I

(ἀνόμους). Meyer's translation fulfills every linguistic and logical condition of the sentence, and represents the view of the best scholars: '*Werdet wie ich;* denn auch ich bin wie ihr geworden.' " Become ye as I; for I also have become as ye." We merely repeat 'have become' (ἐγενόμην) in the second clause from become (γίνεσθε) in the first, and supply the substantive verb. For ' I also' (κἀγώ), equivalent to *I on my part,* compare 1 Cor. 11 : 1. The sense, then, is : " Become in your relinquishment of Jewish rites as I am in that respect; *for I also,* who am a Jew, and consequently attached to such rites by every tie of natural sympathy, have forsaken them, and *become as you are*—that is, have placed myself upon the Gentile ground, which is that of the non-observance of the Jewish Law. It is but reasonable, therefore, that I should ask you (δέομαι ὑμῶν) to concur with me, and thus be simply true to your own natural position, when I, against every bias of birth and education, have cast aside the forms of Judaism, and assimilated to the Gentiles." The other possible explanation would be: " Become as I am, because I also was (once) as ye are (in your present status)—that is, I was under the Jewish Law and was trusting in obedience to it for justification before God, as you now propose to do." But this does not suit the connection as well as the first explanation. **Ye have not injured me at all.** Revised Version: *Ye did me no wrong.* Paul, however grieved with their distrust of his Lord, had no reason to complain of any wrong done to himself. Far from it. He remembered with joy the reception which they gave to him and to his message when he was first among them. They had welcomed him with an open and cordial spirit, with impulsive generosity and confidence.

13. Ye know how through infirmity of the flesh I preached the gospel unto you at the first. The Revised Version is more accurate: *But ye know that because of an infirmity of the flesh I preached the gospel unto you the first time.* Literally : 'the former time,' for he had preached among them at two different times, as we have seen. (1:9.) This verse preserves to us a singularly interesting fact respecting the apostle's ministry. Preach-

ing the gospel in Galatia was not included in the plan for his second missionary journey. But owing to a bodily disease, which is probably alluded to in 2 Cor. 12 : 7, seq., he was constrained to remain for a time in that province where he preached the gospel with great success. We find it impossible to identify his 'infirmity of the flesh ' with any particular form of disease, though it was evidently painful and humiliating. Perhaps it was all the more so, because he could often obtain miraculous healing for others, though not, in this case, for himself. "The thorn in the flesh, a messenger of Satan," was not removed, even at his thrice-repeated prayer, but such grace was given him that ' his strength was made perfect in weakness,' and he was able 'to glory in his infirmities.' It is not indeed demonstrable that he refers to the same infirmity here and in 2 Cor. 12, but it seems exceedingly probable. The two letters were written about the same time, and the language used in both might naturally be applied to one and the same disease.

A few interpreters have urged with much zeal the opinion that it was a disease affecting the eyes, and have appealed to the blindness produced by the light from heaven at his conversion (Acts 9 : 3, 8) as favorable to this opinion. But that blindness, however caused, was healed by miracle (Acts 9 : 17, 18), and it is scarcely probable that this divine cure was imperfect. They have also discovered in Acts 13 : 9; 14 : 9; 21 : 3 a slight indication of imperfect sight, though the same expression is frequently used of those who are not presumed to have weak eyes or a dim sight (see Luke 4 : 20; 22 : 56; Acts 1 : 10; 3 : 4; 6 : 15; 7 : 55; 10 : 4; 11 : 6), and cannot be relied upon as evidence that the apostle's vision was impaired. Reference has also been made in support of this hypothesis to Gal. 4 : 15; 6 : 11, on the ground that *ophthalmia* would account for what is said in both places; but it will appear upon examination that there is no need of this hypothesis to account for the language of either passage. Hence the arguments in support of the conjecture that Paul's "thorn in the flesh " was a painful inflammation and weakness of eyes "seem to melt away under the light of careful examination." (Lightfoot.)

14 And my temptation which was in my flesh ye despised not, nor rejected; but received me as an angel of God, *even* as Christ Jesus.

15 Where is then the blessedness ye spake of? for I bear you record, that, if *it had been possible*, ye would have plucked out your own eyes, and have given them to me.

16 Am I therefore become your enemy, because I tell you the truth?

14 preached the gospel unto you the [1] first time; and that which was a temptation to you in my flesh ye despised not, nor [2] rejected; but received me as an angel of God, *even* as Christ Jesus. Where then is

15 that gratulation [3] of yourselves? for I bear you witness, that, if possible, ye would have plucked out your eyes and given them to me. So then am I be-

16 your eyes and given them to me. So then am I be-

---

[1] Gr. *former*.....[2] Gr. *spat out*......[3] Or, *of yours*.

The conjecture of Lightfoot, supported by a parallel account concerning a malady with which Alfred the Great was afflicted, "that it was of the nature of epilepsy," must not be accepted as more than a conjecture, though it is very ingeniously defended. See note on "St. Paul's Infirmity in the Flesh," p. 169, seq.

14. And my temptation which was in my flesh ye despised not, nor rejected. Revised Version is better: *And that which was a temptation to you in my flesh, ye despised not, nor rejected.* A more literal rendering would be: 'Your trial in my flesh ye despised not, nor spurned' (or loathed). The reading '*your* trial' is much better supported than '*my* trial.'[1] So the apostle's disease appears to have been of such a nature as to test their candor and regard for him, of such a nature that he feared it would destroy confidence and excite disgust. Yet it did not. **But received me as an angel of God, even as Christ Jesus.** That is, they listened to him as if he were a messenger of God to them, as if he were Christ Jesus himself. He could not have been received with more respect; they welcomed his message as divine and himself as Christ's ambassador to them. The apostle recalls their treatment of himself and of his 'good news' with the most cordial gratitude. This is characteristic of him, and in this he is an example which every Christian should seek to follow.

15. Where is then the blessedness ye spake of? The text of this clause is uncertain. If we adhere to the best supported reading, the sense is this: 'Where then is your

self-felicitation? Your boasting of happiness, in view of my presence and preaching among you? Has it vanished so soon? Have you no longer any heart to congratulate yourselves on having the gospel ministered to you, or on having been accepted in Christ and made heirs of God?' But if the other reading be preferred, the sense will naturally be: "Of what sort, then, was your self-felicitation? your calling yourselves happy, because of my ministry of the gospel among you? How shallow and vain it must have been! Or, how strange and inexplicable in the light of your present course!' The former reading and explanation are preferable, we think, to the latter.[2] **For I bear you record that, if it had been possible, ye would have plucked out your own eyes and have given them to me.** Here the Revised Version is more accurate: *For I bear you witness, that, if possible, ye would have plucked out your eyes and given them to me.* The emphasis belongs to the word 'eyes,' not to the pronoun 'your,' and therefore 'own' should not be added in translating the Greek. The 'eyes' are mentioned because of their preciousness. Compare Ps. 17 : 8; Zech. 2 : 8. Paul means to say that the Galatians were at that time ready to do anything in their power for him. Their love was then ardent and apparently free from any tincture of selfishness or suspicion. Notwithstanding his infirmity in the flesh those were blessed days to the apostle, and he feels that a reference to them must touch the hearts of his Galatian children.

16. Am I therefore become your ene-

---

[1] Lachmann, Tischendorf, Westcott and Hort, and the Canterbury Revisers insert 'your' in the text with א * A B D * F G, and the Vulgate and Coptic Versions. Besides, as the more difficult reading, it would not have been likely to take the place of an easier one.

[2] The reading που οὖν is supported by the earliest MSS. א A B C F G P, and is accepted by Tischendorf, Tregelles, Lachmann, Westcott and Hort, Sieffert. Lightfoot and Meyer suppose that the original text was τίς οὖν, since it is easy to see how που could be substi-

tuted for τίς. "especially as several of the Greek commentators who read τίς explain it by που," while it is hard to account for the displacing of που by τίς. Perhaps the great preponderance of manuscript authority should be considered decisive in favor of the easier reading in such a case as this. Yet if it were necessary to adopt the more difficult reading τίς οὖν, the meaning might still be (as Lightfoot insists), " What has become of your rejoicing? Where has it vanished (understanding ἐστί)?"

17 They zealously affect you, *but* not well; yea, they would exclude you, that ye might affect them.
18 But *it is* good to be zealously affected always in *a* good *thing,* and not only when I am present with you.
19 My little children, of whom I travail in birth again until Christ be formed in you,

17 come your enemy, [1] by telling you the truth? They zealously seek you in no good way; nay, they desire
18 to shut you out, that ye may seek them. But it is good to be zealously sought in a good matter at all times, and not only when I am present with you.
19 My little children, of whom I am again in travail

1 Or, *by dealing truly with you.*

---

my, because I tell you the truth? Compare the Revised Version: *So then am I become your enemy?* etc. The apostle discerns in them a change of feeling toward himself as well as toward the gospel which he had always preached, such a change that they treated him as if he were an enemy rather than their spiritual father. 'Because I tell you the truth' is a present or imperfect participle (ἀληθεύων), and might be translated 'by speaking to you the truth,' or even 'by dealing truly with you.' The former is generally preferred, as the apostle had dealt with them as a preacher and teacher, and as speaking truth is the ordinary sense of the word. "To what period does the participle refer? Certainly not (*a*) to the present Epistle, as the apostle could not now know what the effect [of it] would be (Schott); nor (*b*) to the *first* visit, when the state of feeling (ver. 15) was so very different, but (*c*) to the *second* (Acts 18:23), when Judaism had probably made rapid advances." (Ellicott.) That visit took place not long after the scene at Antioch, described in 2:11–21.

17. They zealously affect you, but not well; yea, they would exclude you, that ye may affect them. The Revised Version substitutes 'seek' for 'affect,' 'in no good way' for 'not well,' and 'nay' for 'yea.' There appears to be no sufficient reason for rendering the Greek word (ἀλλά) either 'yea' or 'nay,' for the usual translation 'but' fulfills every claim of the context, thus: *They zealously seek you in no good way, but they desire to shut you out, that ye may seek them.* The word translated 'zealously seek' evidently signifies 'pay court to.' But from what do the Judaists desire to exclude their Galatian adherents? Probably "from other teachers who do not belong to their clique, as Paul and those agreeing with him" (Sieffert), or "from Paul and that sounder portion of the church with which he in thought associates himself." (Ellicott.) We prefer the former, because the word 'them' in the clause 'that ye may seek them' probably refers to them in their role as teachers, and suggests

that those from whom the Judaists wished to exclude their followers were also teachers.

18. But it is good to be zealously affected always in a good thing, and not only when I am with you. If we have correctly explained ver. 17, the Revised Version should also be followed in this: *But it is good to be zealously sought in a good matter at all times, and not only when I am present with you.* Thus Paul approves of their being sought in a good cause, or, better still, in a good way (Ellicott); for they had been sought most earnestly by himself when he was present with them, and they were even now sought by him when he was not present in person, but was making his appeal by letter. According to Sieffert-Meyer the sense is as follows: 'While those Judaists do not seek you in a good way, it is nevertheless good that one be sought in a good cause, and therefore good that ye should be sought by me in good at all times, and not merely when I am with you in person.' No other explanation of the verse is so satisfactory as this. The obvious meaning of the Common Version is very different; namely, that Paul approves of their being zealous themselves in a good cause at all times, and not merely when they are stimulated by his presence. This is unsatisfactory, (1) because it assigns to the verb 'to be zealously affected' a sense which it cannot have in the preceding verse, and (2) because the words 'good' and 'in a good thing' naturally connects this verse with the first clause of ver. 17, and not with the last. Ellicott's translation brings out very clearly the thought of ver. 17, 18: "They pay you court in no honest way; yea, they desire to exclude you, that ye may pay THEM court. But it is good to be courted in honesty AT ALL TIMES, and not only when I am present with you."

19. My little children, of whom I travail in birth again until Christ be formed in you. The Revised Version says: 'I am again in travail' for 'I travail in birth again.' Paul compares his deep solicitude and painful anxiety for the Galatians to the feelings of a

20 I desire to be present with you now, and to change my voice; for I stand in doubt of you.
21 Tell me, ye that desire to be under the law, do ye not hear the law?

20 until Christ be formed in you—yea, I could wish to be present with you now, and to change my voice; for I am perplexed about you.
21 Tell me, ye that desire to be under the law, do ye

mother in travail. He had once before experienced a similar anxiety in their behalf, namely, at the time of their conversion. Now he experiences the same again, as he waits for their return to Christ. This return he speaks of as if it were a new birth. Yet it would be pressing his words unduly to find in them the doctrine of a "second conversion," in the modern sense of the expression. They had indeed turned away from the simplicity of the faith, and had begun to look upon legal works as necessary to salvation. At the same time, as we may safely conclude, the ardor of their love to Christ had diminished. In such circumstances their return to him would be the renewal of their Christian life; and he would then be formed in them, the hope of glory. There is a wonderful tenderness and faith expressed by these words of the great apostle, especially if we ascribe to him in this passage the use of John's endearing word, 'little children.' But there is some reason to doubt whether he wrote this word. It may be due to an error of transcription.[1] Yet the singular fitness of the affectionate diminutive to the context pleads in its support, as well as the possibility that a transcriber may have thought the word 'children' Pauline, and the word 'little children' Johannine. Westcott and Hort, Ellicott, Lightfoot, Sieffert-Meyer, and a majority of scholars retain the diminutive.

20. I desire to be present with you now, and to change my voice; for I stand in doubt of you. The Revision reads: "*Yea, I could wish to be present with you now, and to change my voice; for I am perplexed about you.*" Ellicott translates: "I could indeed wish," etc.—that is, if it were possible, and this represents appropriately what is implied by the imperfect tense of the verb. He feels that they cannot understand him as they would, if he were there speaking to them *viva voce*. If he were with them, he could use more gentleness and less severity. His tone could be changed. And the reason why he could wish this is expressed in the last clause,

"because I am perplexed about you." Literally, '*in* you,' which is not good English, though the preposition '*in*' points to the object or sphere in which his perplexity takes its rise.

CONCLUSION OF THE ARGUMENT BY A BIBLICAL ALLEGORY. (21–31.)—"This second part of the discussion he closes by employing the history of Abraham and his family as an allegory or illustration of the two systems which he has been considering. The subjoined are the main points of the comparison which he institutes here. Judaism, or the legal system, of which Hagar, who was a bondwoman, may be considered as a type, imposes a spiritual bondage on those who adhere to it; whereas Christianity, which is a Free Dispensation, and hence fitly represented by Sarah, who was a freewoman, liberates men from this bondage, and makes them the children of God. Again, as Ishmael was born in a mere natural way, so the Jews are a mere natural seed; but Christians, who obtain justification in conformity with the promise made to Abraham, are the true promised seed, even as Isaac was. Further, as in the typical history, Ishmael persecuted Isaac, the child of promise, so it is not to be accounted strange that, under the gospel, the natural seed, that is, the Jews, should persecute the spiritual seed, that is, Christians. And, finally, as Isaac was acknowledged as the true heir, but Ishmael was set aside, so must it be as to the difference which exists between Jews and believers. The former, or, in other words, those who depend on their own merit for obtaining the favor of God, will be rejected; while those who seek it by faith shall realize the blessing. (4 : 21-23.)" (Hackett).

21. Tell me, ye that desire to be under the law, do ye not hear the law? The word law appears to be used in the first clause of the Mosaic Code, and in the second of the Pentateuch in which that code was written. Those addressed are supposed to be inclined to accept the doctrine of the Judaizing teachers, and to rely upon obedience to the law as

[1] For a number of the best uncials have childen (τεκνα), instead of 'little children' (τεκνία)—e. g., ℵ * B D * F G, while the less important uncials ℵ c A C D b c E K L P, have 'little children' (τεκνία).

22 For it is written, that Abraham had two sons, the one by a bondmaid, the other by a free woman.

23 But he who was of the bondwoman was born after the flesh; but he of the freewoman was by promise.

24 Which things are an allegory: for these are the two covenants; the one from the mount Sinai, which gendereth to bondage, which is Agar.

25 For this Agar is mount Sinai in Arabia, and answereth to Jerusalem which now is, and is in bondage with her children.

22 not hear the law? For it is written, that Abraham had two sons, one by the handmaid, and one by the 23 freewoman. Howbeit the son by the handmaid is born after the flesh; but the son by the freewoman 24 is born through promise. Which things contain an allegory: for these women are two covenants: one from mount Sinai, bearing children unto bondage, 25 which is Hagar. ¹ Now this Hagar is mount Sinai, in Arabia, and answereth to the Jerusalem that now is: for she is in bondage with her children.

---

¹ Many ancient authorities read *For Sinai is a mountain in Arabia.*

---

well as upon the work of Christ as a ground of acceptance with God. Whether 'do ye not hear the law?' means 'do ye not hear it read in your meeting?' or 'do ye not hearken to it, giving ear to what it really says?' is perhaps doubtful. The question, however, is quite as striking, if understood in the former way. In that case, the apostle expresses by it his surprise that they can wish to be under the law after having even heard it read, to say nothing of having penetrated by earnest attention its deeper meaning. In either case, however, the sense is pertinent.

22. For it is written, that Abraham had two sons, the one by a bondmaid, the other by a free woman. Compare Genesis, chapters 16 and 21. The Revised Version is more literal: 'One by the handmaid, and one by the free woman,' the word 'handmaid' being regarded as synonymous with the word 'bondmaid.'

23. But he (who was) of the bondwoman was born after the flesh; but he of the free woman was by promise. Here the Common Version translates 'bondwoman,' instead of 'bondmaid,' in the preceding verse. Uniformity of rendering would have been better. Again, the Revisers have supplied the word 'the son,' instead of 'who was,' and of 'he,' which is an improvement: 'Howbeit the son by the handmaid is born after the flesh, but the son by the free woman (is born) through promise.' The birth of Ishmael had in it nothing indicative of divine intervention, nothing contrary to the course of nature; but that of Isaac was due to the promise of God, and was brought to pass by virtue of that promise, against the ordinary course of nature.

24. Which things are an allegory—or, according to the Revised Version, *contain an allegory*, which seems to be a just interpretation of the original word. For that word signifies to express one thing under the figure of another. "An allegory," says Hesychius,

"suggests something besides what is heard." The expression 'which things' refers not only to the facts of the birth of the two sons, but also to the principal features of the narrative as a whole and in general. **For these are the two covenants**—rather, *these women are, or represent, two covenants*. The 'for' makes this sentence explanatory of the preceding statement. 'Which things contain an allegory; for these women mean two covenants.' Compare Matt. 13 : 39; 26 : 26-28; Gen. 40 : 26, 27. **The one from the Mount Sinai, which gendereth to bondage, which is Agar.** 'The' before Mount Sinai is wrongly inserted by the translators, and the Revised Version is, on the whole, better: *One from Mount Sinai, bearing children unto bondage, which is Hagar.* "The Sinaitic Covenant is allegorically identical with Hagar." (Sieffert-Meyer.)

25. For this Agar is mount Sinai in Arabia. A very difficult sentence, translated as follows in the Bible Union Revision: "(for the word Hagar is Mount Sinai in Arabia)." The article before Hagar in the Greek text is not *feminine*, as it must have been if the reference were to the bondmaid of Abraham, but *neuter*, as if pointing to the word itself, or to its meaning and use in Arabia. The noun Hagar, Paul says, is equivalent in Arabia, or among the Arabs, to the name Mount Sinai. "Paul informs us," says Dr. Hackett, "in Gal. 4 : 25, that one of the names of Sinai in Arabia was Hagar. No other writer mentions such a name, and the apostle may be supposed to have learned the fact during his visit to that country. (Gal. 1 : 17.) This contact between the two passages is certainly remarkable." "'I went into Arabia,' says St. Paul, in describing his conversion to the Gentiles. It is useless to speculate, yet when, in a later chapter of the same epistle, the words fall upon our own ears, 'This Hagar is mount Sinai in Arabia,' it is difficult to re-

25 But Jerusalem which is above is free, which is the
mother of us all.
27 For it is written, Rejoice, thou barren that bearest
not; break forth and cry, thou that travailest not: for
the desolate hath many more children than she which
hath a husband.
28 Now we, brethren, as Isaac was, are the children
of promise.

26 But the Jerusalem that is above is free, which is
27 our mother. For it is written,
    Rejoice, thou barren that bearest not ;
    Break forth and cry, thou that travailest not :
    For more are the children of the desolate than
        of her who hath the husband.
28 Now ¹we, brethren, as Isaac was, are children of

1 Many ancient authorities read ye.

sist the thought that he, too, may have stood
upon the rocks of Sinai, and heard from Arab
lips the often repeated 'Hagar,'—'rock,'—
suggesting the double meaning to which the
text alludes." (Stanley, "Sinai and Palestine,"
p. 50.)¹ And answereth to (the) Jerusalem
which now is—or the present Jerusalem.
'Answereth'—is in the row or rank with,
stands in the same category with. But what
is the subject of this verb? Is it 'one' (covenant) from Mount Sinai, or Mount Sinai
where the covenant was established, or Hagar
the bondwoman who is figuratively identical
with the covenant and with Sinai? The next
clause is an argument in favor of holding the
subject of this verb to be Hagar. For she is
in bondage. The Revised Version of that
clause is correct; namely, for she is in bondage with her children. The present Jerusalem
with her children are the Jewish people in
bondage to the law, just as Hagar was in
bondage with her children.²

26. But (the) Jerusalem which is above
is free. We insert the article from the Greek
text before Jerusalem, in order that the contrast between 'the Jerusalem which now is'
and 'the Jerusalem which is above' may be
fully preserved. In his Epistle to the Philippians, Paul declares that "our citizenship is
in heaven" (3:20); in the Epistle to the Hebrews it is written: "but ye are come unto
mount Zion, and unto the city of the living
God, the heavenly Jerusalem" (12:22); and in
the Book of Revelation it is said: "I will
write upon him the name . . . of the city of
my God, the new Jerusalem, which cometh
down out of heaven from my God." (3:12.)

Compare 21 : 2. 'The Jerusalem above' is
therefore a figurative expression, equivalent
to the heavenly Jerusalem or the new Jerusalem, conceived of as the home of believers in
Christ. Which is the mother of us all—
more accurately: which is our mother; for
the word 'all' is an addition to the original
text. In the Hebrew idiom, a city is spoken
of as the mother of her citizens. Her condition is theirs, and their condition is hers.
They are born in her, and are often called in
a collective sense her 'daughter.' (Isa. 52:2;
62:11; Jer. 4:31; 6:3; Micah 4:5.)

27. For it is written, Rejoice, thou
barren, that bearest not: break forth
and cry, thou that travailest not: for the
desolate hath many more children than
she which hath a husband. Addressed to
confirm the preceding statement that the free
Jerusalem is our mother. The last clause is
translated as follows in the Revised Version:
"for more are the children of the desolate
than of her which hath the husband"; and
by the Bible Union Version: "because many
are the children of the desolate, rather than
of her who has the husband." Hence the
meaning must be either that, while both
have children, those of the former are 'many'
but those of the latter are not; or that, while
both have children, those of the former are
many, even more than those of the latter.
The words are quoted from the Greek Version
of Isaiah 54:1, a passage whose Messianic character was generally admitted. It is the Jerusalem above, the New Covenant, represented in
the allegory by Sarah, that is to be so fruitful.

28. Now we, brethren, as Isaac was,

¹ Yet the text is doubtful. Instead of τὸ γὰρ (א C F
G K L P), τὸ δὲ is found in several of the best MSS. But
the meaning of the sentence is about the same whichever conjunction is preferred. Tischendorf has the
former, Westcott and Hort the latter. Again, "Ἀγὰρ
is read before Σινᾶ in A B D E K L P, but is wanting in
א C F G and the later Fathers. On internal as well as
external grounds, it seems necessary to consider this
word a part of the text as it came from the hand of

Paul. For the MSS. in favor of the insertion are decid-
edly superior to those in favor of the omission of "Ἀγὰρ,
and the reading is also a more difficult one.

² The reading 'for,' instead of 'and,' is required by
the best MSS. (א A B C D * F G P) and several of the
early revisions (Sahidic, Memphitic, Syriac Peschito),
and with this reading the natural subject of the verb is
'the present Jerusalem.'

29 But as then he that was born after the flesh persecuted him *that was born* after the spirit, even so *it is
now.*

30 Nevertheless what saith the Scripture? Cast out
the bondwoman and her son: for the son of the bondwoman shall not be heir with the son of the free woman.

31 So then, brethren, we are not children of the
bondwoman, but of the free.

29 promise. But as then he that was born after the
flesh persecuted him *that was born* after the Spirit,
30 even so it is now. Howbeit what saith the Scripture? Cast out the handmaid and her son: for the
son of the handmaid shall not inherit with the son
31 of the freewoman. Wherefore, brethren, we are not
children of a handmaid, but of the freewoman.

---

are the children of promise. A more precise rendering of the Greek text would omit
'the' before 'children.' And it is also note-
worthy that 'promise' is rendered emphatic
by the position which is given it in the sentence. The Bible Union Revision follows another text, and translates the verse: 'But ye,
brethren, after the manner of Isaac, are children of promise.'[1] The essential meaning of
the verse is the same whichever pronoun is
correct. There is, however, some reason on
the ground of textual authority to prefer 'ye,'
and this direct application of the thought to
the Galatians must be pronounced very natural and forcible.

**29. But as then he that was born after
the flesh persecuted him that was born
after the Spirit, even so it is now.** The
language of this verse probably refers in the
first instance to Gen. 21 : 9, where Sarah is
said to have seen Ishmael 'mocking,' or, literally, *laughing.* Perhaps the laughter was
mocking laughter. "As Abraham had laughed
for joy concerning Isaac, and Sarah had
laughed incredulously, so now Ishmael laughed
in derision, and probably in a persecuting
and tyrannical spirit." (Bp. Harold Browne,
in the "Bible Commentary.") Compare Gen.
21 : 6 and Ezek. 23 : 32. The tense of the verb
'persecuted' (ἐδίωκεν) represents the action as
in progress or continuous, not as completed;
and it is conceivable that Paul regarded the
event described in Gen. 21 : 9 as only the first
manifestation of a hostility which had been
characteristic of the Ishmaelite line ever since.
Compare Ps. 83 : 7; 1 Chron. 5 : 10, 19. 'Born
after the flesh' means born in a natural manner; 'born after the Spirit' means born in a
supernatural manner—that is, in accordance
with a promise given and fulfilled by the
Spirit of God. It is plain that Paul looked
upon the extraordinary birth of Isaac as hav-

ing its counterpart in the regeneration of men
by the Spirit of God.

**30. Nevertheless what saith the Script-
ure? Cast out the bondwoman and her
son: for the son of the bondwoman shall
not be heir with the son of the freewoman.**
The words of Sarah quoted in this verse are
called 'the Scripture,' or what 'the Scripture
saith,' as if they were a disclosure of the
divine will. (Gen. 21 : 9.) And this they certainly were; for, though grievous to Abraham
(see ver. 11), they were distinctly approved
by Jehovah (ver. 12): "In all that Sarah saith
unto thee, hearken unto her voice; for in
Isaac shall thy seed be called." The import
of this in Paul's discussion is very plain. Not
only are those who simply trust in Christ
without the works of the law accepted and
justified by God, but those who rely upon
legal ordinances and service for divine favor
are rejected. The law must give place to the
gospel; Judaism must be severed from Christianity. Those who are insisting with fanatical zeal upon the necessity of circumcision to
salvation, are Ishmaelites, not Israelites, sons
of the bondwoman and not sons of the freewoman. Yet at this very time the Judaizing
party in the churches of Palestine was preter-
naturally active and apparently successful.
How absolute was the apostle's confidence in
the truth of his gospel!

**31. So then, brethren, we are not chil-
dren of the bondwoman, but of the free.**
A better text is followed by the Revisers:
Wherefore (διό, instead of ἄρα), *brethren, we are
not children of a* (not 'the') *handmaid (bondwoman), but of the freewoman.* 'A bondwoman' is equivalent to *any* bondwoman, because there are many legal systems by which
men are kept in bondage. '*The* freewoman,'
because there is but one covenant of promise,
represented in the allegory by Sarah. How

---

[1] This text is supported by excellent manuscripts
(B D * F G 6. 17. 61. 67 ** and others), though not by the
most important early versions. Lachmann, Tischendorf, Tregelles, Sieffert-Meyer, Ellicott, Lightfoot, Boise,
and many others accept the reading 'ye,' but Westcott
and Hort, with the Canterbury Revisers, prefer 'we.'
It is difficult to decide between these readings, but the
occurrence of the first person plural in verses 26 and 31
may have led transcribers to change the 'ye' into 'we'
in this intervening verse.

CHAPTER V.

STAND fast therefore in the liberty wherewith Christ hath made us free, and be not entangled again with the yoke of bondage.

1 For freedom did Christ set us free; stand fast therefore, and be not entangled again in a yoke of bondage.

highly did the apostle prize the freedom of Christian life and hope!

Here may be found the last step in Paul's argument for the gospel as revealing a perfect way of life. The remainder of his Epistle is more practical than argumentative or controversial. But it is no less instructive on that account: it is full of thought, some of which is complementary to what has been already written.

Ch. 5: "The apostle here exhorts the Galatians to maintain their liberty in Christ, because the surrender of it would deprive them of all benefit from the gospel, and render them debtors to keep the whole law in order to be saved. (1-6.) He reminds them of the sad contrast between their present state and the commencement of their Christian career; cautions them against the danger even of incipient error, and reminds them how absurd it was to appeal to his own example in excuse for their perversion of the rite of circumcision. (7-12.) He expresses the wish that those who were misleading them might be cut off from all connection with them, and be accounted as outcasts and heretics. (12.) He then turns to warn them against an abuse of their Christian liberty, enjoins upon them an observance of the law as a rule of duty, the essence of which is love, and the requirement of which in that respect they would be enabled to fulfill by following the dictates of the Spirit. (13-18.) To enable them to judge whether they are actuated by the Spirit, or an opposite principle, he enumerates, first, some of the works of the flesh, and then the characteristic fruits of the Spirit. (19-26.)" (Hackett.)

1-6. THE GALATIANS EXHORTED TO MAIN-

TAIN THEIR FREE CHRISTIAN STATUS, AND NOT BY CIRCUMCISION TO BIND THEMSELVES TO KEEP THE WHOLE LAW.

1. Stand fast therefore in the liberty wherewith Christ hath made us free, etc. This translation follows a Greek text, not so well supported by manuscript authority as the text followed in the Revised Version: *With freedom did Christ set us free; stand fast therefore,* etc. Still better is the marginal rendering, 'For freedom,' etc.[1] And the word 'freedom' is emphatic. For *freedom,* and not for pupilage or any inferior state, did Christ set us free. His deliverance of us from bondage to the law was for the purpose of establishing us in the family of God as sons and heirs. Yet none of these translations, except the first, preserves the article before 'freedom,' though it belongs to the original text. Paul evidently refers to the liberty of which he has been speaking in the previous chapter—that is, Christian liberty, and his meaning would be more exactly expressed by retaining the article and inserting an explanatory phrase: 'For the freedom' [of sons and heirs] 'did Christ set us free.' The same result might be secured by translating the article *this:* 'For this freedom did Christ set us free.' But it is, perhaps, better to forego perfect clearness of statement than to purchase it by an addition to the original text, or by a free rendering of the article. To introduce his exhortation, the apostle gathers up into a single sentence the result of his discussion, giving the place of emphasis to the word 'freedom': 'With (or, for) the freedom (just spoken of) did Christ set us free; stand fast, therefore, and be not entangled again in a yoke of bondage.'[2] 'Entangled,' or, *ensnared,* is sometimes used with reference to a

---

[1] *Für die Freiheit hat uns Christus befreit,* is Weizsäcker's translation. Compare Buttmann (Thayer's), pp. 178, 179.

[2] The text of the first clause is by no means certain, yet the reading approved by the Revised Version, Westcott and Hort, Tischendorf, Meyer, Schaff, and others, is sustained by a clear preponderance of testimony. It differs from the Textus Receptus by placing οὖν after στήκετε instead of ἐλευθερίᾳ, by having no relative ᾗ, and by reading ἡμᾶς χριστὸς instead of χριστὸς ἡμᾶς. The οὖν is not found in the first clause after ἐλευθερία

in ℵ A B C* D E F G P and many cursives, or in the Vulgate, Memphitic, Sahidic, Armenian, Gothic, or Syriac (Peschito) Versions. Only Cc K L and many cursives have it. Nearly the same manuscripts and versions have this conjunction after στήκετε. The relative ᾗ is wanting in ℵ A B C D* P and present in Dbetc K L and many cursives. It is easy to see how this relative might be inserted by a transcriber for the sake of rendering the language of the apostle more perspicuous.

2 Behold, I Paul say unto you, that if ye be circumcised, Christ shall profit you nothing.

3 For I testify again to every man that is circumcised, that he is a debtor to do the whole law.

4 Christ is become of no effect unto you, whosoever of you are justified by the law; ye are fallen from grace.

2 Behold, I Paul say unto you, that, if ye receive 3 circumcision, Christ will profit you nothing. Yea, I testify again to every man that receiveth circumcision, 4 cision, that he is a debtor to do the whole law. Ye are [1] severed from Christ, ye who would be justified

---

1 Gr., *brought to nought.*

---

net in which one is caught and held; and here a yoke of religious bondage is evidently conceived as something in which the Galatians were liable to be caught and held captive. Formerly they had been in bondage to the superstitious fears and rites of heathenism; now they were in danger of accepting the no less useless and burdensome ritual of Judaism. They were moving in the wrong direction, away from spiritual liberty into spiritual slavery, and the apostle's heart is deeply moved with anxiety to preserve them from so great a calamity.

2. Behold, I Paul say unto you, that if ye be circumcised, Christ shall (*will*) profit you nothing. In their circumstances, submission to circumcision would involve a relinquishment of their faith in Christ, a virtual confession that he was not an all-sufficient Saviour, "the way and the truth and the life," and a return to works of law as being the only ground of acceptance with God. It may be assumed that they would not entertain the thought of being circumcised, unless they were led to suppose they could not be saved without it, and so were led to trust in obedience to the law for salvation; and Paul saw that, if they were to do this, they would be in a more hopeless condition than they were before hearing the gospel. By the words, 'I Paul,' the apostle assumes a right to speak with authority, and shows that he expects his authority to have some weight with those addressed.

3. For I testify again to every man that is circumcised, that he is a debtor to do the whole law. Observe the changes in the Revised Version—'yea' instead of 'for,' and 'receiveth circumcision' instead of 'is circumcised.' In both cases the Revision is an improvement. The apostle is speaking to the point. Every Galatian Christian who allows himself to be circumcised undertakes by that act to obey the whole Jewish Law, moral and ceremonial. For that law in its origin and purpose is a unit, and he that confesses his obligation to obey one part of it admits his

obligation to obey every part of it. He that trusts for salvation in his obedience to any requirement of the law, makes his salvation depend on obedience to every requirement of the law. "For whosoever shall keep the whole law, and yet stumble in one point, is become guilty of all." James 2 : 10, Revised Version; compare Gal. 3 : 10. The adverb 'again' implies his utterance of the same truth before, probably when he was last with them (1 : 9); if not at that time, then in this Epistle. See 3 : 10.

4. Christ is become of no effect unto you, whosoever of you are justified by the law. It is difficult to make a satisfactory translation of the first clause. The Revised Version reads: 'Ye are severed from Christ.' The Bible Union Version: 'Ye are separated from Christ.' Dr. Davidson: "Ye were separated from Christ." It is better, however, to render the Greek verb in this clause by the English perfect tense: 'Ye have been separated from Christ'—that is, your separation from Christ is a completed act in the case of those of you who are seeking to be justified in law. There is no article before the original word for 'law,' and though the Jewish Law be meant, it is thought of as standing for all divine law; and the meaning is this, that one who is now resorting to law for justification has thereby severed his connection with Christ. Hence, Paul employs the tense of completed action in the next clause: **Ye are fallen from grace.** And this is as much as to say, by your first movement toward the legal system, toward a reliance upon works of law for acceptance with God, you have surrendered in principle your confidence in Christ as the ground of hope. The apostle has in view their standing before God as fixed by a logical interpretation of their conduct. By that conduct they turn away from salvation through grace, and sink back into the condition of men who are seeking to work out a righteousness of their own. What Christ himself may yet do for them in his great mercy is not said, but the

5 For we through the Spirit wait for the hope of righteousness by faith.
6 For in Jesus Christ neither circumcision availeth any thing, nor uncircumcision; but faith which worketh by love.
7 Ye did run well; who did hinder you that ye should not obey the truth?

5 by the law; ye are fallen away from grace. For we through the Spirit by faith wait for the hope of
6 righteousness. For in Christ Jesus neither circumcision availeth anything, nor uncircumcision; but
7 faith ¹working through love. Ye were running well; who did hinder you that ye should not obey

---

¹ Or, wrought.

---

attitude which they are taking toward his work for them is faithfully shown. Hence, the apostle is not teaching in this passage the modern doctrine of "falling from grace," whatever may be the bearing of the entire Epistle on the truth of that doctrine.

5. For we through the Spirit wait for the hope of righteousness by faith. The connective 'for' make this verse confirmatory of the preceding statement. (ver. 4.) The fact that true Christians await in faith the fulfillment of their hope is an evidence that one who is turning to legal works for salvation has fallen away from the method of grace. 'The hope' cannot here mean the feeling of hope, because true Christians are not 'waiting for' that; they already possess it. It must rather signify that which is hoped for, the object of hope. But this hoped-for good is in some way defined by the words 'of righteousness.' What then does the word righteousness here signify? It may either denote a perfect moral character as that which is hoped for, or it may denote acceptance with God through Christ, which is the pledge of that which is hoped for, that is, eternal life. In other words, it may signify either righteousness or justification. And as the latter meaning is suggested by the whole previous argument, as well as by the sense of the corresponding verb in the foregoing verse, we adopt it here. Thus this verse teaches that eternal life, for which Christians wait in hope, belongs to justification and will eventually flow from it; that this justification and hope are dependent on faith in Christ; and that this faith itself is due to the work of the Holy Spirit: an exceedingly rich cluster of truths, every one of which is a protest against the Judaistic movement among the Galatians.

6. For in Jesus Christ neither circumcision availeth anything, nor uncircumcision; but faith which worketh by love. Union with Christ is the only condition of acceptance with God. Obedience to the Jewish Law has no power to help one who is in fellowship with Christ; heathenism has as

little. Faith is the one indispensable thing, and faith, if genuine, works by love; that is to say, it exerts itself, puts forth its energy by means of love to Christ, to Christians, and to men. Faith, indeed, has great power, and through the channel of love it lays hold of God and man. "It is as much as to say," remarks Luther, "he that will be a true Christian indeed, . . . must be a true believer. Now he believeth not truly if works of charity follow not his faith. . . . Paul, therefore, in this place sets forth the whole life of a Christian man; namely, that inwardly it consisteth in faith toward God, who hath no need of our works; and outwardly in our charity or good works toward men, whom our faith profiteth nothing."

This verse is often alleged in proof of Paul's radical agreement with James. For the faith which he describes as the root of the new life is an energetic working principle; it is not only a hand opened to receive, but also a hand opened to give; if it has boundless capacity for trust, it has equal capacity for love. The passage has also been alleged in proof of the slight importance of any outward rites, even though appointed by Christ. But without reason; for the apostle makes no reference to Christian duties or ordinances, and love, without which faith is dead, insists upon obedience to the commands of the Master who is loved. Ritual observances as expressions of faith must not be confounded with ritual observances as works of righteousness on which the soul relies for justification.

7-12. He Deplores their Leaning towards Judaism, but has Confidence that they yet Abide in the Truth, and Will Cast Out the Leaven of False Teachers.

7. Ye did run well: who did hinder you that ye should not obey the truth? The imperfect tense of the Greek verb 'to run' is more exactly rendered in the Revised Version: *Ye were running well.* As Paul looks back over their Christian course pre-

E

8 This persuasion *cometh* not of him that calleth you.
9 A little leaven leaveneth the wh le lump.
10 I have confidence in you through the Lord, that
ye will be none otherwise minded: but he that troubleth you shall bear his judgment, whosoever he be.

8 the truth? This persuasion *came* not of him who
9 calleth you. A little leaven leaveneth the whole
10 lump. I have confidence to you-ward in the Lord,
that ye will be none otherwise minded: but he that
troubleth you shall bear his judgment, whosoever

vious to the arrival of Judaizing teachers
among them, he can speak of it with praise.
They were doing their work bravely. They
were mindful of the truth which he had
preached to them, and were seeking to grow
in the grace and the knowledge of Christ.
But a change was now manifest. They were
no longer pressing forward in the way of life.
And so he asks with some surprise and perhaps
indignation : ' Who is it that has cut off your
way and arrested your progress (compare 1
Thess. 2 : 18; Rom. 12 : 22; 1 Peter 3 : 7), so
that ye should not hearken to the true gospel?'
Some one's persuasion had evidently been
more effective with them than that of the
truth itself, as preached by Paul, and by
others who accepted his views of the gospel.

**8. This persuasion cometh not of him
that calleth you.** A literal translation would
read : *The persuasion is not from him that
calleth you.* That is, the persuasion to which
I have just referred, and to which you have
hearkened, instead of hearkening to the truth,
is not from God who calls you from darkness
to light. The word 'persuasion' may be
either active or passive; it may signify the act
of persuading, or the result of that act, being
persuaded. Here it is commonly and correctly supposed to be active, especially because
of its connection with 'him that calleth.'
How dangerous this 'persuasion' might be the
apostle now shows by an illustration.

**9. A little leaven leaveneth the whole
lump.** What is represented here by 'a little
leaven'? Many answer, false teaching; and
others, false teachers. The former insist that
the influence of erroneous teaching is more
like the influence of leaven than is the influence of false teachers. But the latter insist
that the context directs the mind to a small
company of teachers, and that their work
would diffuse itself through the churches as
leaven diffuses its energy through the whole
mass. We incline to the latter view, but do
not see that the meaning of the passage would
be essentially different if the former were
intended. The latter, however, throws a little
more emphasis on the *personal* element, and

we think it highly probable that the zeal of
the Judaizers, even more than the plausibility
of their teaching, was effective in spreading
their influence.

**10. I have confidence in you through
the Lord, that ye will be none otherwise
minded.** Better: *I have confidence in regard
to you in the Lord*, etc. The pronoun 'I' is
emphatic: I myself, whatever others may say
or think, have confidence in you. 'In the
Lord' is added by the apostle because the
source of his confidence as to the future belief
of the Galatians is in Christ. The second
clause, 'that ye will be none otherwise
minded,' seems to mean that ye will think
and feel as I have expressed myself in regard
to this matter. In saying this he may have
had in mind the context from ver. 7 to ver.
9 inclusive, which shows that the Judaists had
led the Galatians away from the truth in a
dangerous manner, or he may have had in
mind the proverb just quoted, believing that
they would agree with him as to the danger
suggested by it. In either case, he is confident
that his Galatian brethren, forewarned and
instructed, will agree with his view and, resisting the teachers of error, regain their trust in
Christ alone for salvation. **But he that
troubleth you shall bear his judgment,
whosoever he be.** Literally, 'the judgment'
which his sin merits. The word 'troubleth'
signifies to disturb the mind or the community.
Both these evils were no doubt occasioned by
the new teaching which contradicted that of
the apostle. Even the ardent, impulsive, unstable Galatians were not likely to be carried
over to Jewish legalism without a sharp struggle in the minds of individuals or without
loud controversy in the churches. 'Shall bear
his judgment' is a clear recognition of divine
government and justice. The teacher of false
doctrine, however conspicuous he may be,
will not escape retribution. The ringleader
of this proselyting raid is accountable to God,
and at his tribunal will surely be made to bear
a heavy burden of displeasure. Yet there
may be no reference to any particular leader.
The singular may perhaps be used merely for

12 As many as desire to make a fair shew in the
flesh, they constrain you to be circumcised; only lest
they should suffer persecution for the cross of Christ.

13 For neither they themselves who are circumcised
keep the law; but desire to have you circumcised, that
they may glory in your flesh.

12 mine own hand. As many as desire to make a fair
show in the flesh, they compel you to be circumcised: only that they may not be persecuted ² re-
13 the cross of Christ. For not even they who ² receive circumcision do themselves keep ³ the law;
but they desire to have you circumcised, that they

1 Or, *by reason of*......2 Some ancient authorities read *have been circumcised*......3 Or, *a law.*

generally inserted in his epistles, and which
consisted usually of a few words written by
himself. His mode of referring to this mark
or sign, so *I write* (οὕτω γράφω), shows that it
was some peculiarity by which his hand was
readily distinguished from that of the ordinary amanuensis. That peculiarity, as appears
from the epithet (πηλίκοις, *how great*) in our
epistle, was the size of the written characters
or letters, for which (οὕτω γράφω, *so I write*) he
was well known. Whether Paul wrote the
whole Epistle with his own hand, or the last
verses only; whether he wrote in so peculiar
a way from want of practice, and hence, awk-
wardness; and whether he alludes to the
matter because he would authenticate the
letter, or to remind the Galatians of his earnestness and painstaking in their behalf, are
questions which do not affect the translation,"
and were not, therefore, considered by Dr.
Hackett in the article from which this extract
is made. But in the American Edition of
Smith s "Bible Dictionary," he remarks:
"The rendering of the Authorized Version
—'How large a letter I have written with
mine own hand (Gal. 6:11)—might lead us to
suppose that in that instance, at least, he de-
parted from his usual practice. But the
correct translation removes that impression,
showing that the remark applies rather to a
few words or verses only of the letter as the
customary token of authenticity." (Page 759.)

**12. As many as desire to make a fair
show in the flesh.** 'In the flesh' here means
in matters pertaining to the physical nature
and outward life. Ritualism was the sphere
in which they sought to shine. The forms of
godliness were more to them than the reality.
And underneath their zeal for Jewish cere-
monies was a desire to be considered very
religious themselves—at least, in the eyes of
their countrymen. **They constrain** (or,
compel) **you to be circumcised.** Of course,
by insisting that without circumcision men
could not be saved. In so far as this conviction could be implanted in the minds of the
Galatians, they would be compelled by it to

submit to the Jewish ritual, and especially to
the decisive initiatory act. **Lest they should
suffer persecution for** (or, *Only that they
may not be persecuted for*) **the cross of
Christ.** These Judaizing teachers were,
therefore, men who claimed to be Christians,
and who were influenced to do as they did by
a strong desire to avoid the reproach and persecution which the Jews directed, with all
bitterness, against those who forsook the law
of Moses to trust in the cross of Christ for
salvation. According to the inspired judgment of Paul, they were influenced by a desire
to stand well with their countrymen, and especially by a desire to escape persecution from
them. Thus the apostle pours a flood of light
upon the motives of these Judaizing teachers.
In the next verse, he justifies this judgment in
respect to their motives by an appeal to one
feature of their conduct. 'For the cross' (τῷ
σταυρῷ) is used to express the occasion or reason
of the persecution. Compare Rom. 11 : 20,
30 and 2 Cor. 2 : 13, and Winer p. 210ᶜ.

13. For neither they themselves, etc.
Better: *For not even do they themselves who
receive circumcision keep the law.* Two questions must here be answered: 1. In what tense
is the participle, in the present (περιτεμνόμενοι,
who receive circumcision) or in the perfect
(περιτετμημένοι)? The reasons which make for
the opinion that it is present are: (1) That
it is the more difficult reading. (2) That it is
fairly well attested; namely, by B (F G) L,
and many cursives. For the former reason
chiefly we feel constrained to look upon the
present tense as probably genuine, and the
perfect as a correction. But who are intended
by those 'who receive circumcision'—the
Gentile Christians or the Judaizing teachers?
If the former are intended, we must suppose
that some of the Galatian Christians were
already submitting to circumcision, but without keeping the law in all respects, or even
expecting to keep it. But this is scarcely
probable. It would have been an illogical
and untenable position for sincere men. Besides, the subject of this clause is evidently

CHAPTER I.

I WAS born in Licking county, Ohio, October 19, 1837. I moved to Sangamon county, Ill., in the spring of 1843. My father and mother died, respectively, in 1845 and 1846. I was about nine years old when these events occurred. I then lived with relatives, and worked for various parties till the war of the Rebellion broke out in 1861.

MY ENLISTMENT.

I voted for Lincoln in 1861, little thinking we should be in the midst of a terrible war so soon, although it had been threatened by the South. I always did believe that if we had principles they ought to be so good that we should be willing to die for them if necessary. I said that if we must have war in order to allow the majority to rule in this country, it would have to come; I would support my principles by taking up arms, if nothing else would do.

I was married to Miss Laura A. Cowgill, February 7, 1861. I enlisted at Ottawa, Ill., in what became afterwards Company E, Twenty-sixth Illinois Volunteer Infantry, and was sworn into the service at Camp Butler, Springfield, Ill., July 22, 1861.

ENGAGEMENTS.

OUR company was detached from the regiment and encamped to guard a bridge on Salt River, Mo., during

CHAPTER III.

Bewilderment—Hunting a Location—Description of the Prison—Conversations with Captors—New Adventures and Experiences.

ON entering the prison the sight that met my gaze was the most horrible that my mind could have pictured. I have already referred to the appearance of the prisoners and my feelings as I saw them from a distance; but upon entering the prison we were met by a thousand or more of living forms that seemed to be mere human skeletons, among whom we had come to dwell. They had learned of our coming, and were gathered near the gate (which was the prison market-place) to trade and offer to us, for money, whatever articles they had to sell.

TATTERED AND TORN.

SOME had one leg of their pantaloons worn off to the knee; some had both knees and the remainder of the legs of their clothing tattered into strings; some had both shirt-sleeves gone, up to the shoulder; many had neither hat nor cap, and but few of them wore shoes. They were dirty and greasy, and their faces, hands and bodies were covered with pitch and dirt gathered from burning bituminous pine; and the whole multitude looked worse than any set of coal-miners that I had ever seen coming out of the earth in their mining garments.

old axes, or anything that could be at all utilized for making progress in the work. The dirt was drawn up to the surface in pieces of blankets, canvass or whatever else would serve the purpose. The ropes were strips of canvass, blankets or other material that could be used with any success. Under these disadvantages few cared to undertake the labor necessary to dig a well. Along the bank of the creek some had dug surface-holes, about two feet deep, but the water from them came from the filthy bottom-lands, and was but little better than that in the creek. Still, as I have before stated, the great majority of the prisoners used the creek water from the time the stockade was finished (which must have been early in the spring) till September. While the upper water was thus utilized for drinking and cooking, the creek was also used by the prisoners for bathing and washing clothing. Some tried to perform the latter work, during the warm weather, by wading in and sousing the garments in the running stream; but without soap their labors were not generally successful, and the custom did not extensively prevail.

There were prisoners in Andersonville from the various prisons in the South. Some of them had been prisoners for more than twelve months, and still wore the same clothing in which they were captured, or what was left of it, and there were rags hanging upon them that had never been washed.

With reference to the creek water, besides the prisoners bathing and washing their clothing in it, inside the prison, there was the whole rebel camp on the outside, above us, washing, bathing, watering horses and using it for whatever purpose they chose. In addition

ing in the creek. The guard had shot him through the head without the slightest warning—not for crossing the dead-line, but for standing on the crossing, leaning over it, and dipping up water from the danger-side.

The guards were selected, partially, from boys under age and old men, who were enrolled as state militia, and not considered eligible for the regular service. We were told, and it was generally believed, that a guard was given a furlough to go home for every prisoner whom he shot for violating rules that had a death-penalty attached for their infraction. This regulation, the rebels said, was an inducement for vigilance on the part of the guards, and to prevent the escape of the prisoners. These boy-guards, especially, deemed it a great honor to kill a "Yank," and then go home, strut about, and boast of it. It caused them to be indeed very vigilant —in some instances as watchful as a hungry hawk in search of a chicken to devour; and with anything like an excuse, as in the case of the man on the crossing, they would shoot.

After I was removed to Florence prison, I found a similar arrangement for crossing the creek. The rebels, I suppose, had determined that it was not safe to have so many of us crossing so near the dead-line, but they gave us no warning when the change was made. I went down, early one morning, for water, but just as I was about to pass over the plank, another prisoner stepped on it before me. At that instant I saw one of the boy-guards, who was stationed near by, raise his gun to shoot him. In alarm I shouted to the man, and he jumped off in time to save his life. Others also came to cross over, but I stood there, as long as I could, to warn them off. The guard raised no objec-

had heard that a tunnel was being dug, and sent in a message that no rations would be issued until some one revealed where it was located, or until it was found. It was not probable that any person knew where to locate the tunnel except the company of ten or twelve who were interested in the enterprise; nevertheless they threatened to starve 10,000 helpless men for the acts of a few. We had drawn our scanty rations the night before the cold weather came upon us, had eaten the last of them the next morning, and were waiting, with great anxiety, for the usual rations; but when the time came, instead of provisions, we were informed of the rebels' fatal decision to withhold them. For three days, less six hours, not a thing did we have to eat, besides being desperately hungry at the commencement.

At night each would lie down in his quarters, good or bad—many resting upon the bare ground, with nothing but a blanket over them. Others, who had neither quarters nor blankets, dug holes on the side of the hill, into which they crept and lay all night, in their rags, on the cold ground. Some, who had strength enough, moved about to keep warm; but the wind was so chilly and strong that they could neither walk about all night, nor rest comfortably anywhere.

In the morning, after the sun had been up sufficiently long to heat the ground, all these destitute ones would crawl out and seek some favorable place in the sunshine where they could warm up their cold bodies and stiffened limbs. With starvation doing its work, suffering from intense hunger, they sat, by hundreds and thousands, in gloom, watching the declining sun, feeling the cool air that denoted another cold night,

ROBBERY.

These were among the principal speculations carried on by enterprising parties. After the order came not to sell any rations, I thought, on one occasion, I would bake one-half of my day's ration of meal into a cake and go down on the market and trade it for meal, at a profit. There was no law against exchanging goods in this manner. It was a nice cake for that place. I could hardly keep from eating it, I was so hungry. I soon found a man who wanted to buy it. I told him I dare not sell it. He said no one would know it, and offered me a fair price for it. He had it in his hand, looking at it. I was tempted to violate the law, even with so severe a penalty as was attached to it, and concluded it would probably be all right. I consented. Immediately he told me he would keep the cake, and not pay me anything for it, and if I said one word he would call a policeman and have me taken to the whipping-post. I dared not protest—and he walked off with my cake.

Some will read this and deem it a small affair; but no doubt I felt as chagrined at the time, and under the circumstances, as many a one would if robbed of quite a sum of money.

11 And I, brethren, if I yet preach circumcision, why do I yet suffer persecution? then is the offence of the cross ceased.
12 I would they were even cut off which trouble you.
13 For, brethren, ye have been called unto liberty; only use not liberty for an occasion to the flesh, but by love serve one another.

11 he be. But I, brethren, if I still preach circumcision, why am I still persecuted? then hath the
12 stumblingblock of the cross been done away. I would that they who unsettle you would even [1] go beyond circumcision.
13 For ye, brethren, were called for freedom; only use not your freedom for an occasion to the flesh, but through love be servants one to another.

[1] Or, mutilate themselves.

emphasis, and the application be to every one who was engaged in pressing circumcision on the Galatians.

11. And I, brethren, if I yet preach circumcision, why do I yet suffer persecution? then is the offence of the cross ceased. Or (Revised Version), *But I, brethren, if I still preach circumcision, why am I still persecuted? then hath the stumbling-block of the cross been done away.* The connection of this verse with the preceding is obscure. But it may be supposed that Paul was reminded by his strong language concerning Judaists, that he had been himself accused by them of conceding the necessity of circumcision, for example, in the case of Timothy, and that he now proposes by one decisive argument to prove the absurdity of the charge. 'But as to myself, brethren, if it is circumcision that I still preach, as I certainly did before my conversion, why am I notwithstanding this persecuted?' For to my persecutors the only stumbling-block pertaining to the cross, or to the gospel, is its dispensing with obedience to the law as a means of justification; and if I so preach it as to include in it obedience to the law as necessary to acceptance with God, the stumbling-block is removed, and their hostility to me becomes inexplicable.

12. I would that they were even cut off which trouble you. The Greek interpreters all understand this of self-mutilation. "Would that they who unsettle you would even mutilate themselves." (Davidson.) So understood, the language is an instance of just sarcasm. Let those zealots for a fleshly rite who resort to desperate misrepresentation in defense of it, go the whole figure and make themselves eunuchs, like the priests of Cybele. "Circumcision under the law and to the Jews, was the token of a covenant. To the Galatians, under the Gospel Dispensation, it had no such significance. It was merely a bodily mutilation, as such differing rather in degree than in kind from the terrible practices of the heathen priests." (Lightfoot.)

13-15. PAUL EXHORTS THEM NOT TO ABUSE THEIR CHRISTIAN FREEDOM BY NEGLECTING TO OBEY THE LAW OF LOVE.

13. For, brethren, ye have been called unto liberty. By the word 'for' this statement is made to justify the sharp language of the previous verse. 'I cannot, as you perceive, look upon these Judaistic "subverters," who are creating dissension and bringing you under a yoke of bondage, without deep indignation; for ye were called by the grace of God unto freedom in Christ his Son.' Yet, while justifying all he had said against the advocates of circumcision and the Jewish Law, the apostle feels the need of cautioning the brethren in Galatia against an abuse of their Christian liberty. Perhaps he knew that some had already begun to turn their liberty into license; and, therefore, he adds, **only use not liberty for an occasion to the flesh.** Whether 'use' should be supplied in English to bring out the full sense of the Greek, or some other verb, like *make*, is somewhat doubtful; but looking at the Greek sentence, we prefer 'make' (ποιεῖτε): 'Make not your freedom into an occasion for the flesh'—meaning by 'the flesh' the entire sinful nature of man. Thus the apostle "at once hastens, with more than usual earnestness, to trace out the ineffaceable distinction between true spiritual freedom and a carnal and antinomian license." (Ellicott.) That 'the flesh' here means the whole sinful nature of man is evident from the following paragraph. (Ver. 16-26.) **But by love serve one another.** An exhortation of deep and far-reaching import, reminding us of a wonderful scene at the close of our Lord's ministry, when he taught his disciples to render the humblest service to one another. See John 13 : 4-16. The word translated 'serve,' signifies to render bondservice; and as it is in the present tense, it denotes continuous serving; so that the Revised Ver-

14 For all the law is fulfilled in one word, *even* in this; Thou shalt love thy neighbour as thyself.

15 But if ye bite and devour one another, take heed that ye be not consumed one of another.

16 *This* I say then, Walk in the Spirit, and ye shall not fulfil the lust of the flesh.

17 For the flesh lusteth against the Spirit, and the Spirit against the flesh: and these are contrary the one to the other; so that ye cannot do the things that ye would.

14 For the whole law is fulfilled in one word, *even* in this; Thou shalt love thy neighbour as thyself.

15 self. But if ye bite and devour one another, take heed that ye be not consumed one of another.

16 But I say, Walk by the Spirit, and ye shall not 17 fulfil the lust of the flesh. For the flesh lusteth against the Spirit, and the Spirit against the flesh; for these are contrary the one to the other; that ye

sion gives the sense correctly, 'Through love be servants one to another.' 'You can do the humblest work with the utmost freedom of spirit, if you do it for the benefit of your brethren and under the blessed influence of love.' No man ever perceived the beauty and energy of love with a more distinct vision than the writer of this Epistle.

14. For all the law is fulfilled in one word—that is, by observing one precept. The Greek verb is in the perfect tense, and therefore the apostle teaches that whoever has done what is required by the single command which he has in mind, has obeyed the whole law. Of course, he does not intend to affirm that any one has done this, but only that doing this involves doing the rest. **Even in this; thou shalt love thy neighbour as thyself.** See Lev. 19 : 18; Matt. 22 : 39; Luke 10 : 27; Rom. 13 : 9, 10. To obey this command one must have perfect love to his neighbor, and such love cannot exist in a heart that is not filled with supreme love to God. The excellence of the gospel is seen in this, that by it love to God and man is implanted in the heart as it never is by the claims of law; so that by driving men from itself to Christ, for pardon and peace, the law gets an honor and love that it can obtain in no other way. As a rule, for those who have begun to love God, the law is not only holy, but also good; while as a means of salvation for sinners it is powerless. Compare Rom. 7 : 12; Gal. 3 : 21.

15. But if ye bite and devour one another, etc. "He says not simply *bite*, which indicates sudden anger, but *devour*, which implies continuance in an evil mind." Again, "Strife and contention are destruction to those who introduce them, as well as to those who welcome them." (Chrysostom.) The more sacred and intimate the fellowship disturbed, the more difficult is it to restore harmony. "A brother offended is harder to be won than a strong city; and such contentions are like the bars of a castle." (Prov. 18 : 19, Rev. Ver.) But

there is some reason to believe that Paul, by his prompt and powerful defense of the gospel, together with his earnest delineation of a true Christian life in contrast with a life of sin, arrested the influx of error and restored the churches to harmony in the truth.

16-26. CONTRAST BETWEEN A LIFE CONTROLLED BY THE FLESH AND A LIFE CONTROLLED BY THE SPIRIT: THE FORMER UNCHRISTIAN, THE LATTER CHRISTIAN.

16. This I say then—more exactly, *Now I say* (Revised Version), or, *mean*. **Walk in the Spirit.** Better, *Walk by the Spirit* —that is, under the guiding impulse of the Holy Spirit, and so in conformity with his will. **And ye shall not fulfil the lust of the flesh.** The double negative in the Greek may be properly rendered, as in the Revised Version, *ye shall by no means fulfil the lust of the flesh*. The word 'flesh' does not here signify the bodily part of man, to the exclusion of his spirit, but his sinful nature—that is, his entire nature before conversion, and whatever is sinful in his nature after conversion. According to Thayer's "Lexicon," it "denotes mere human nature, the earthly nature of man apart from divine influence, and, therefore, prone to sin and opposed to God." The word translated 'lust' signifies 'desire,' 'longing,' 'craving,' and especially, 'desire for what is forbidden.' Compare Rom. 7 : 7, 8; James 1 : 14, 15. When, as in this place, the context shows that it is used in the latter sense, it may properly be translated 'lust,' although the reader must bear in mind that it has no special reference to sensual craving.

17. For the flesh lusteth against the Spirit, and the Spirit against the flesh; and these are contrary the one to the other. A confirmation of the foregoing statement. The desire of man's heart before conversion, and of his remaining evil nature after conversion, is opposed to every impulse of the Spirit, and in acting against the work

18 But if ye be led of the Spirit, ye are not under the law.

19 Now the works of the flesh are manifest, which are these, Adultery, fornication, uncleanness, lasciviousness,

18 may not do the things that ye would. But if ye are 19 led by the Spirit, ye are not under the law, Now the works of the flesh are manifest, which are these, for-

of the Holy Spirit, may be said to oppose the Spirit himself. Hence the apostle adds the sentence, 'and these are contrary the one to the other.' According to the better textual documents (א⁹ B D* E F G against א° A Cᶜ K L P), the true reading is 'for,' instead of 'and.' 'The flesh lusts against the Spirit and the Spirit against the flesh, because they are contrary,' etc. So that ye cannot do the things that ye would—or (Revised Version), that ye may not do the things that ye would. The probable meaning of the clause, when compared with Rom. 7 : 15, 16, is that the opposition of sinful desire arrests the better choice 'so that' it is not carried into effect. It will also be noticed that the verb 'lusteth' is not expressed after the word 'Spirit.' Many interpreters would, therefore, supply a word of similar import, but less associated with evil, such as 'contends,' or 'strives.' Yet this is both unnecessary and unnatural. Compare Luke 22 : 15, "With desire I have desired to eat this passover with you before I suffer." As to the force of the Greek word (ἵνα), translated 'so that,' see Buttmann's "Grammar," 239, who argues that it may be translated so that in a number of passages. Winer, Meyer, and Fritzsche insist upon the telic sense. Dr. Hackett maintains that the telic sense may be retained here. "The apostle predicates the teleological aim here of the 'flesh' (σάρξ), or sinful principle in man, which, according to a correct anthropology, is viewed as the ascendant influence before the beginning of a new life, and after that, as still striving to maintain its ascendency." After having said that the two principles are thus arrayed against each other, he goes on to adjust the sequel of the sentence to that posture of the conflict: "They are opposed to each other, I say, and the danger is that you will remain under the old domination—the flesh, in this struggle with the Spirit, striving to bring it about that you should not do the things which the Spirit has taught you to approve." etc. Meyer and Ellicott understand that each of these principles strives against the other, that you should not do the things which you would do, or will. In case you would do what is approved by the

Spirit, you are prevented by the flesh to the extent of its power; and in case you would do works of the flesh, you are prevented by the Spirit's influence. This is certainly conceivable, bearing in mind the personification of the flesh and the personality of the Spirit; but it seems to me a less natural thought than the one expressed by 'so that,' etc.

18. But if ye be led of the Spirit (are led by the Spirit), ye are not under the law —or, under law. For the article is wanting in the original text, and need not here be supplied in translation. In this verse the apostle declares that the influence of the Spirit is of such a nature as to deliver one from bondage to the law as a means of justification. Animated by that influence, he is truly free, and does the will of God under the impulse of love. Hence, the fact that one is led by the Spirit renders it certain that he is not under law. Moreover, it is evident from a comparison of this verse with ver. 16 and 17, that the law is conceived of as in some way arousing the selfish nature of man into controlling action, while the Spirit inspires him with gratitude and benevolence. The former may beget fear and remorse on the one hand, or self-righteousness and pride on the other; but it does not produce the fruit of trust or love or personal devotion, while the latter produces these, and thereby weakens, if it does not destroy, self-righteousness, pride, and fear.

19. Now the works of the flesh are manifest, which are these—or, 'of which class are' the following. The apostle does not aim to give a full list of sinful works, but specimens which are well known to his readers. This enumeration is translated more correctly in the Revised Version than in the Common Version, thus: Fornication, uncleanness, lasciviousness, idolatry, sorcery, enmities, strife, jealousies, wraths, factions, divisions, heresies, envyings, drunkenness, revellings, and such like—a black catalogue of sins issuing from a selfish heart! Compare the words of Jesus in Matt. 15 : 19, "For out of the heart come forth evil thoughts, murders, adulteries, fornications, thefts, false witness, railings: these are things which defile

20 Idolatry, witchcraft, hatred, variance, emulations, wrath, strife, seditions, heresies,

21 Envyings, murders, drunkenness, revellings, and such like: of the which I tell you before, as I have also told *you* in time past, that they which do such things shall not inherit the kingdom of God.

22 But the fruit of the Spirit is love, joy, peace, long-suffering, gentleness, goodness, faith,

20 nication, uncleanness, lasciviousness, idolatry, sorcery, enmities, strife, jealousies, wraths, factions, divisions,

21 parties, envyings, drunkenness, revellings, and such like: of the which I ¹ forewarn you, even as I did ¹ forewarn you, that they who practise such

22 things shall not inherit the kingdom of God. But the fruit of the Spirit is love, joy, peace, longsuffer-

---

1 Or, *tell you plainly*.

---

the man." Bengel divides these sins into those 'committed (1) with one's neighbor; (2) against God; (3) against one's neighbor; (4) on one's self.' Lightfoot groups them in the same way as (1) *sensual passions*—'fornication,' 'uncleanness,' 'licentiousness'; (2) *unlawful dealings in things spiritual*—'idolatry,' 'witchcraft'; (3) *violations of brotherly love*—'enmities,' . . . 'murders'; (4) *intemperate excesses*—'drunkenness,' 'revellings.' The word 'fornication' appears to signify, in this place, illicit sexual intercourse in the case of those married or of those unmarried; 'uncleanness,' impurity of profligate living, including pederasty; and 'lasciviousness,' open wantonness of conduct, bold defiance of moral order—for example, in the case of whoremongers and harlots. 'Idolatry' denotes the open recognition and worship of false gods, and 'sorcery' the use of magical arts, many of which were practiced in secret. The specifications following these need no explanation; they are sins which spring from selfishness and produce contention, division, and weakness in the churches. I would translate the words 'enmities, strife, jealousy, wraths, intrigues, divisions, factions, envyings, murders, drunkenness, revellings.' The word translated 'wraths' appears to denote 'outbursts of wrath.'[1] The last two nouns, 'drunkenness' and 'revellings,' differ in that the latter is more comprehensive in meaning. It generally includes the former, though it may be

sometimes used where there is no complete intoxication. **Of the which I tell you before, as I have also told you in times past** (*forewarn you, even as I did forewarn you*): **that they which do** (*practise*[2]) **such things shall not inherit the kingdom of God.** 'Even as I did forewarn you' refers to what he had said during his second visit to the churches of Galatia, when some of these 'works of the flesh' had begun to appear among them. 'Shall not inherit,' etc. Whatever may be the relation of men to the church, however loud their profession of faith in Christ, they will perish at last, if their works are such as those just enumerated. They that are of the flesh cannot please God, nor can they "partake of eternal salvation in the Messiah's kingdom"; for they are not sons of God through faith in Christ Jesus, since the faith which they profess to have does not work through love. See ver. 6.

22. But the fruit of the Spirit. Sieffert holds, against Meyer, that "the collective singular, 'fruit,' is intended to fix attention on the inner unity of 'the fruit of the Spirit,' as contrasted with 'the works of the flesh,' which spring out of many different desires." **Is love, joy, peace, longsuffering, gentleness, goodness, faith.** The Revised Version substitutes 'kindness' for 'gentleness,' and 'faithfulness' for 'faith'—in both cases an improvement: in the former, because the Greek word (χρηστότης) signifies 'kindness'

---

1 The word for 'murders' is not found in the Sinaitic and Vatican MSS., or in five cursives. But it is in A C D E F G K L P, and most cursives; also in both forms of the Syriac, the Memphitic, the Armenian, Æthiopic, Gothic, and Vulgate Versions; and is accepted by Lachmann, Meyer, the Revisers. Compare Rom. 1: 29. "The fact, however, of the same alliteration occurring in another epistle written about the same time, is rather in its favor, and the omission in some texts may be due to the carelessness of a copyist transcribing words so closely resembling each other. The reading must, therefore, remain doubtful." (Lightfoot.)

2 A distinction ought to be made in translation between

ποιεῖν and πράσσειν, though the words are of similar meaning. "Roughly speaking, ποιεῖν may be said to answer to the Latin *facere*, or the English *do*—πράσσειν, to *agere*, or English, *practise*. Ποιεῖν, to designate performance; πράσσειν, intended, earnest, habitual performance. Ποιεῖν, to denote merely productive action; πράσσειν, definitely directed action. Ποιεῖν, to point to an actual result; πράσσειν, to the scope and character of the result. In Attic, in certain connections the difference between them is great; in others, hardly perceptible." (Schmidt.) "The words are associated in John 3: 20, 21; 5: 29; Acts 26: 9, 10; Rom. 1: 32; 2: 3; 7: 15, seq.; 13: 4." (Thayer.)

23 Meekness, temperance: against such there is no law.
24 And they that are Christ's have crucified the flesh with the affections and lusts.
25 If we live in the Spirit, let us also walk in the Spirit.
26 Let us not be desirous of vainglory, provoking one another, envying one another.

23 ing, kindness, goodness, faithfulness, meekness,
24 temperance: against such there is no law. And they that are of Christ Jesus have crucified the flesh with the passions and the lusts thereof.
25 If we live by the Spirit, by the Spirit let us also
26 walk. Let us not be vainglorious, provoking one another, envying one another.

1 Or, *self-control.*

or 'graciousness,' rather than 'gentleness,' though gentleness may be included in kindness; and in the latter, because the context requires us to think of a quality which has respect to human relations.

23. Meekness, temperance. *Self-control* is a better rendering of the Greek word for 'temperance.' If there be any special reference to moderation in the use of food or drink, this reference must be inferred from an assumed contrast between this word and the words 'drunkenness' and 'revellings' in ver. 21, and not from any such limitation in the meaning of the word itself. The most that can safely be said is this, that self-control fairly embraces thorough 'temperance' in the use of food and drink. Neither food nor drink of any kind should be used in such a manner as to injure health of body or of mind. **Against such there is no law.** They are all good, and not evil. The law is *for* them, not *against* them. "If ye are led by the Spirit, ye are not under law." (Ver. 18.) "Law is not made for a righteous man, but for the lawless and disobedient," etc. (1 Tim. 1 : 9, 10.) Yet it approves all that is right, though it cannot produce it in fallen man.

24. And they that are Christ's have crucified the flesh with the affections and lusts. The Revised Version is preferable, *And they that are of Christ Jesus have crucified the flesh with the passions and the lusts thereof.* Yet the word 'thereof' might properly be stricken off, because unnecessary to the sense and representing no word in the original. The verb 'have crucified' expresses a completed act, referring, without doubt, to their conversion. At that time they died with Christ that they might live unto God. See 2 : 19, 20; 3 : 26, 27. "To Christians ideally

considered, as here, this ethical mortification of the flesh is something already accomplished (compare Rom. 6 : 2-14); but in reality, it is also renewed continually (Rom. 8 : 13; Col. 3 : 5), though the latter fact is not mentioned in this place." (Meyer.)

25. If we live in (or, *by*) the Spirit, let us also walk in (*by*) the Spirit. Let the outward life agree with the inward. If the latter is moved and directed by the Spirit of God, the former should be controlled by the same divine influence. But that is not an influence which operates without regard to human freedom. No Christian will be kept in the narrow way, unless it be by his own consent and choice. The exhortation means watchfulness, prayerfulness, and effort. The Greek verb for 'walk' is not the same in this verse and in ver. 16. The one used here suggests the idea of an orderly procedure, perhaps of moral and religious conduct regulated by a settled purpose.

26. Let us not be desirous of vainglory, provoking one another, envying one another. If we give to the Greek word translated 'be' its usual signification, the first part of this verse must be translated, '*Let us not become vainglorious,*' as if that were a sin to which Christians were liable, but of which the Galatians had not in any marked degree been guilty. A conceited, vainglorious person is certain to provoke others to dislike and criticize him. At the same time, he is liable to be envious of those who receive the attention and respect which he imagines to be due to himself. It is, therefore, very difficult to preserve brotherly love in churches where some are puffed up with pride, thinking of themselves more highly than they ought to think. See Rom. 12 : 3.

CHAPTER VI.

BRETHREN, if a man be overtaken in a fault, ye which are spiritual, restore such a one in the spirit of meekness; considering thyself, lest thou also be tempted.

2 Bear ye one another's burdens, and so fulfill the law of Christ.

1 Brethren, even if a man be overtaken ¹in any trespass, ye who are spiritual, restore such a one in a spirit of meekness; looking to thyself, lest thou 2 also be tempted. Bear ye one another's burdens,

1 Or, *by*.

Ch. 6: "He adds in the last chapter several general directions, such as relate, for example, to the spirit with which Christians should admonish those who fall into sin, the patience which they should exhibit toward each other's faults, the duty of providing for the wants of Christian teachers, and, in short, performing unweariedly every good work, with the assurance that in due time they should have their reward. (1-10.) He warns them once more against the sinister designs of those who were so earnest for circumcision, holds up to their view again the cross of Christ as that alone in which men should glory, and closes with a prayer for them as those whom he would still regard as brethren. (11-18.)" (Hackett.)

1-10. GENERAL EXHORTATIONS AND WARNINGS.

1. Brethren. This word must be regarded as a spontaneous, unstudied expression of the apostle's feeling toward the Galatians. Though he had reproved and admonished them sharply, he still loves them as brethren in the Lord, and addresses them with deep affection. Thus love pleads when argument is exhausted. If (Revised Version, *even if*) **a man be overtaken in a fault.** The meaning of the verb (προ-λημφθῇ), translated 'be overtaken,' is considered doubtful. It may signify (as καταλαμβάνω, in John 8 : 4), 'be detected,' or, 'surprised '—that is, in the act of transgression. This interpretation is approved by Ellicott, Lightfoot, and others. If correct, the case supposed by the apostle is one which admits of no doubt as to the offense—that is, as to the certainty of its having been committed. Others believe that the verb describes its subject as involved, before he is fully aware of it, in transgression. He is taken, when off his guard by temptation; and, before he clearly apprehends his condition, lapses into wrongdoing; so that his offense is less culpable than it would have been had he acted deliberately. It is difficult to decide which of these significations best suits the context; but, on account of the passage in John, we prefer the former. The offense referred to (παράπτωμα) is, "a lapse from truth and uprightness." In the Revised Version it is rendered 'trespass,' and Fritzsche says that it differs "in figure," but not "in force," from the Greek word (ἁμάρτημα), which denotes a sinful deed. **Ye which are spiritual.** Thus the apostle assumes that there were those in the churches of Galatia who were led by the Spirit of God, and who, under the influence of that Spirit, might deal wisely with offenders. But he does not exhort those who were unconscious of bearing 'the fruit of the Spirit' (5 : 22. 23) to undertake this delicate and difficult task of restoring a brother that has been guilty of known sin. **Restore such a one in the spirit of meekness.** The Revised Version 'in *a* spirit of meekness' answers perfectly to the original. A spirit of meekness is a disposition distinguished by that quality and produced by the indwelling of the Holy Spirit. See 5 : 23. A proud or contentious spirit would utterly disqualify one for the service contemplated by the apostle in this exhortation. **Considering thyself, lest thou also be tempted.** "The transition from the plural to the singular gives the charge a direct personal application : each one of you individually." (Lightfoot.) The word 'also' shows that the 'fault,' or lapse into sin, spoken of in the first clause, is occasioned by temptation, and that even spiritual men are liable to be overcome by temptation. "Let him that thinketh he standeth take heed lest he fall." (1 Cor. 10 : 12.) A consideration of one's own weakness will prevent harsh dealing with an offending brother. This general direction of Paul is perfectly consistent with the more detailed method of procedure laid down by Christ in Matt. 18 : 15-18. The aim in both cases is restoration, not excision; though the latter must follow if the former fails.

2. Bear ye one another's burdens, and so fulfil the law of Christ. Not only should Christians possess a sympathetic spirit which

3 For if a man think himself to be something, when he is nothing, he deceiveth himself
4 But let every man prove his own work, and then shall he have rejoicing in himself alone, and not in another.
5 For every man shall bear his own burden.
6 Let him that is taught in the word communicate unto him that teacheth in all good things.

3 and so fulfil the law of Christ. For if a man thinketh himself to be something, when he is nothing, he
4 deceiveth himself. But let each man prove his own work, and then shall he have his glorying in regard
5 of himself alone, and not of ¹ his neighbour. For each man shall bear his own ² burden.
6 But let him that is taught in the word communi-

I Gr. the other.......2 Or, load.

enters into the condition and shares the sorrow of a trespassing brother, but their mutual love, sympathy, and helpfulness should embrace all the cares and sorrows of the spiritual brotherhood. The love of all the members of a Christian church to one another should be like that which Christ has for them. For this evidently is 'the law of Christ' referred to by the apostle. "This is my commandment, that ye love one another, even as I have loved you." (John 15 : 12.) Compare 1 John 2 : 7-11. Though the Fourth Gospel was not yet written, it is evident that Paul knew the substance of the Lord's sweet and wonderful command to his disciples.

3. For if a man think himself to be something, when he is nothing, he deceiveth himself. This verse confirms the preceding by showing the evils of an opposite spirit and life. He that imagines himself to be strong and able to stand alone, when in fact he is weak in faith and love, deludes himself. Conceit is not only unsympathetic, it is also unchristian and delusive. The man whose piety is not in his life, but in his imagination, is subject to a fatal but cherished error. Faith that does not work by love will not be recognized as genuine at the last day.

4. But let every man prove his own work. As 'but' indicates, the proving of one's own work, here recommended, is neglected by the man who thinks that he is something when he is nothing. "By their fruits ye shall know them" is a rule that can be applied to ourselves as well as to our neighbors. And it is easier for a Christian to test his *work* by the law of love than it is for him to test his whole spiritual condition by that law. For the work is a definite outcome from his inner life; it is positive, voluntary, and in a sense visible; he can look at it, measure it, weigh it, prove its quality, and go back with it as a lamp into the still, obscure depths of the soul which he could scarcely enter without it. Compare 1 Cor. 11 : 31. The remainder

of the verse is more accurately rendered in the Bible Union Revision: "*And then shall he have [the] ground of glorying in reference to himself, and not to another.*" For the Greek word (καύχημα) has the article, and does not signify 'rejoicing,' but rather 'the ground of glorying'; here, the ground of glorying which the character of his own work furnishes. Compare the words of Paul in 1 Cor. 4 : 5: "And then shall every man have his praise from God"; literally, "the praise from God" —that is, the praise due to each. But in this place the apostle has in mind what a Christian man should deem an occasion for exultant thankfulness; it is the service or suffering which, by the grace of God, he is himself enabled to bear; it is his work tested by the law of love, and not his work as compared with 'the other' Christian's work, which may be of the poorest quality. Ellicott's interpretation is excellent: "If any one wishes to find matter for boasting, let it be truly searched for in his own actions, and not derived from a contrast of his own fancied virtues with the faults of others." Compare 2 Cor. 10 : 17; 11 : 30; 12 : 9. In the next verse is a statement of the reason for this method of proving one's own work.

5. For every man shall bear his own burden. Dr. Hackett proposes to translate this verse as follows: 'For each one shall carry his own load,' remarking that "the burdens which the apostle urges his readers to 'bear' (ver. 2) are the faults and offenses of others, toward which we are required to be tolerant, charitable; and the 'load' which every one has to 'carry' is that of his own accountability for all his sins and deficiencies, be it as it may with others, whether they are more or less guilty than himself."

6. But. This particle is omitted in the Common Version. It belongs, however, to the text and must be considered in the interpretation. Giving it, as usual, a slightly adversative sense, the connection of thought is

7 Be not deceived; God is not mocked: for whatsoever a man soweth, that shall he also reap.
8 For he that soweth to his flesh shall of the flesh
reap corruption; but he that soweth to the Spirit shall
of the Spirit reap life everlasting.

7 cate unto him that teacheth in all good things. Be
not deceived; God is not mocked: for whatsoever
8 a man soweth, that shall he also reap. For he that
soweth unto his own flesh shall of the flesh reap
corruption; but he that soweth unto the Spirit

as follows: 'But,' though in the matter referred to, each one will carry his own load, it should not be so in everything, **let him that is taught in the word communicate unto him that teacheth, in all good things.** A more literal rendering would be: 'let him that is taught . . . go shares with him that teacheth in all good things.' Compare 1 Cor. 9: 11: "If we have sown unto you spiritual things, is it a great thing if we shall reap your carnal things?" If the word translated 'let him participate with' (κοινωνείτω) is pressed to its utmost extent, it may be taken to mean that members of a Christian church should consider their property as a possession common to themselves and their religious teachers. But this cannot be the apostle's meaning. All that his words imply is that the laborer is worthy of his hire, that one who gives his time and strength to the religious instruction of others should receive from them the worldly things necessary to health and appropriate to one in his condition. See 1 Thess. 2: 6, 9; Phil. 4: 10-18; 1 Tim. 5: 17, 18. Some have supposed that 'in all good things' must refer to spiritual possessions, and that the apostle exhorts the people who are still in need of religious instruction to be partakers in all divine knowledge with their teachers, by eagerly listening to their words and becoming familiar with all they know. But this thought is less suited to the context than the other. For the exhortations of the preceding paragraph show that the Galatians were deficient in mutual love, sympathy, and helpfulness, and these deficiencies are closely allied to neglect of those who served them in the gospel. Compare also the use of the same verb in Phil. 4: 15 and Rom. 12: 13. In the former, Paul says that "no church communicated with me as concerning giving and receiving but ye only"; and in the latter, "distributing (communicating) to the necessities of the saints." Compare 1 Cor. 9: 11. It is also said that all the Greek Fathers who interpret the passage give it the meaning adopted by us.

The apostle proceeds now to enforce what he has just said by an appeal to the divine law of retribution, thus taking up again from an-

other point of view, and with a far-reaching glance into the future, the thought of ver. 4.

7. Be not deceived. Paul uses the same admonition elsewhere, with reference to what immediately follows it. See 1 Cor. 6: 9; 15: 33. So also here. **God is not mocked** —that is, with impunity. Contemptuous treatment of him is sure to bring evil on those who are guilty of it. The very laws of their nature are his servants, doing his will. Yet every act of sin expresses contempt for his being, authority, and judgment. It will therefore bring upon the sinner a punishment answering to his sin. **For whatsoever a man soweth, that shall** (or, *will*) **he also reap.** This is one of the profoundest testimonies of Scripture as to the moral government of God. There is nothing arbitrary in that government. Retribution will be proportioned to sin, and will be seen to grow out of it with a terrible certainty. "They would none of my counsel, they despised all my reproof. Therefore shall they eat of the fruit of their own way, and be filled with their own devices." (Prov. 1: 30, 31.) But the same principle obtains in the direction of good as well as of evil.

8. For he that soweth unto his (*own*, Revised Version) **flesh shall of the flesh reap corruption.** By 'his own flesh' is meant his own sinful nature, and by 'sowing unto' it must be meant making it the seed plot or ground which he cultivates, and from which his life proceeds; in other words, it is suffering his sinful nature to rule his conduct —nay, it is adopting its influence as the rule of his life. And, therefore, the harvest is 'corruption,' moral worthlessness and decay, the ruin of soul and body forever. **But he that soweth to the Spirit shall of the Spirit reap life everlasting.** Paul does not say 'to his own Spirit,' thus setting the higher principles and powers of man's nature over against the lower, and tracing the harvest of eternal life to man himself; but he says, 'to the Spirit,' thus testifying that a true Christian counts all his right-living a fruit of divine grace in his soul. He yields himself to the influence of the Holy Spirit, and strives with that Spirit to overcome and destroy the

9 And let us not be weary in well doing: for in due season we shall reap, if we faint not.

10 As we have therefore opportunity, let us do good unto all *men*, especially unto them who are of the household of faith.

11 Ye see how large a letter I have written unto you with mine own hand.

9 shall of the Spirit reap eternal life. And let us not be weary in well-doing; for in due season we shall

10 reap, if we faint not. So then, [1] as we have opportunity, let us work that which is good toward all men, and especially toward them that are of the household of the faith.

11 See with how large letters I [2] write unto you with

---

1 Or, *since*......2 Or, *have written*.

---

influence of the flesh. And the harvest is 'everlasting (or, *eternal*) life'! Not merely endless existence in some unknown condition, —out of harmony, perhaps, with God and his universe,—but *life*, full, free, pure, joyous, progressive, in fellowship with God, and at home with all his friends; this, and whatever better is conceivable, is embraced in the meaning of 'eternal life,' as used by the sacred writers.

9. And let us not be weary in well doing; for in due season we shall reap, if we faint not. 'In due season'—in its own fitting time, we shall be put in possession of this eternal life. Let us not, then, faint in the way. The words remind us of the apostle's testimony respecting himself not far from the time when this letter was written. "Wherefore we faint not; but though our outward man is decaying, yet our inward man is renewed day by day. For our light affliction, which is for the moment, worketh for us more and more exceedingly an eternal weight of glory," etc. (2 Cor. 4 : 16-18.)

10. As we have therefore opportunity, etc. Here again, as in a great majority of instances where they differ, the Revised Version is more accurate than the Common Version. *So then, as we have opportunity, let us work that which is good toward all men, and especially toward them that are of the household of the faith.* 'So then' (ἄρα οὖν) is an expression peculiar to Paul: the former showing that the following words agree with something just said, and the latter, that they are a conclusion from that something, 'accordingly therefore.' 'As we have opportunity'—whenever we have a suitable occasion. 'Let us work that which is good.' It is desirable to translate the verb here used 'work,' in order to distinguish it from another, which must be translated 'do' (ἐργάζομαι, 'work'; ποιέω, 'do'). 'Toward all men.' The apostle teaches the same doctrine as his Lord, the doctrine of universal philanthropy and, as far as possible, of universal beneficence. See 1 Tim. 3 : 1-4;

Matt. 5 : 44-48; 22 : 39; Luke 10 : 29-37. The 'opportunity' of doing good to foreigners and strangers is comparatively rare, but the disposition to do them good may be constant. Moreover, it is well to bear in mind that facilities of travel and intercourse, are rapidly multiplying the opportunities which Christians have of doing good to all men. 'And especially unto them who are of the household of faith.' Thus all believers in Christ are represented as belonging to one family, and are urged to cultivate a family affection by rendering assistance to one another. In this respect also, the apostle simply reiterates the teaching of his Lord. His exhortation is but the statement, in another and practical form, of the Saviour's 'new commandment,' which was, at the same time, as old as the spiritual nature of man. For that those who are one in spirit and aim and hope should be bound together by special affection, and should make special efforts to benefit one another, is natural, inevitable. The extraordinary love of the early Christians to one another was a surprise to the heathen, and was, in many cases, the principal thing which recommended the new religion to their attention, and compelled them to see in it a beneficent power.

With this beautiful sentiment, the apostle finishes the main body of his Epistle to the Galatians. All that remains is an earnest résumé of what he has said, a brief reference to himself, and a final benediction.

11-16. BRIEF RECAPITULATION.

11. Ye see how large a letter. Better, *See with how large letters I have written unto you with mine own hand.* "If we accept the results of the present exegesis," says Dr. Hackett, "we must translate in this way . . . There is a harmony between this verse, as thus correctly understood, and 2 Thess. 3 : 17, which may be worth pointing out. In the Epistle to the Thessalonians, Paul speaks of the salutation there as added by his own hand, and as being a sign (σημεῖον) or attestation of the genuineness of the letter—such, in fact, as he

14 But God forbid that I should glory save in the cross of our Lord Jesus Christ, by whom the world is crucified unto me, and I unto the world.
15 For in Christ Jesus neither circumcision availeth any thing, nor uncircumcision, but a new creature
16 And as many as walk according to this rule, peace be on them, and mercy, and upon the Israel of God.

14 may glory in your flesh. But far be it from me to glory, save in the cross of our Lord Jesus Christ, through ¹ which the world hath been crucified unto me, and I unto the world. For neither is circumcision any thing, nor uncircumcision, but a new
16 ² creature. And as many as shall walk by this rule, peace be upon them, and mercy, and upon the Israel of God.

1 Or, whom.......2 Or, creation.

the subject of the next clause, and the subject of that clause must be the Judaizing teachers. The Greek expression 'who receive circumcision' (οἱ περιτεμνόμενοι) denotes the party practicing and advocating circumcision; and the present participle is used to describe their conduct in its present moral effect. Yet they do not keep the law in all its parts themselves. **But they desire to have you circumcised, that they may glory in your flesh.** For by making proselytes to Judaism they would gain the approval of their countrymen, without renouncing their confidence in Christ. The mere outward conformity of Gentile Christians to the Jewish Law in the initiatory rite, through their influence, would furnish them matter for boasting among the Jews, something to which they could appeal as evidence of their fidelity to the law. Thus they were selfish and hypocritical, seeking their own ends while professing to seek for the salvation of the Gentiles. Certainly the Galatians would do themselves irreparable harm if they should give heed to the counsels of such men.

14. But God forbid that I should (*far be it from me to*) **glory, save in the cross of our Lord Jesus Christ, by whom** (*through which*) **the world is** (*hath been*) **crucified unto me, and I unto the world.** The expression 'far be it' (μὴ γένοιτο) is always employed by the apostle to declare his horror at or repugnance to some doctrine or act. So here, the thought of glorying in anything save the cross of Christ is represented as shocking to his mind. And by 'the cross of Christ' he certainly means the propitiatory death of the Redeemer. In that he was ready to glory and exult forever, but in nothing else. In that was to be found pardon and peace, victory over sin, and eternal life in the age to come. There is a slight ambiguity in the word translated 'which,' as the form of the Greek relative must be the same whether it refers to 'the cross' or to the 'Lord Jesus Christ.' Indeed,

the same pronoun would be used if Paul intended it to represent the complex idea of 'the cross of Christ.' Perhaps we cannot do better than to give it this wider reference, and if so the rendering of the Revised Version 'through which' is correct. It was then through the propitiatory death of Christ upon the cross that Paul felt himself to be dead unto the world, and the world dead unto him. By this double expression he seeks to emphasize his utter abandonment of sinful aims, his entire separation from all that does not belong to Christ, his profound indifference and even opposition to every ceremonial which turned him away from the Lord Jesus. And as a reason for this he adds the following statement:

15. For in Christ Jesus neither circumcision availeth anything, nor uncircumcision, but a new creature (or, *creation*). Why then does the apostle oppose circumcision so earnestly? Because it was insisted upon as a means of acceptance with God, as one of the legal works on which salvation depends,— though it has no power to give the new life in Christ which is the beginning and the pledge of eternal peace. He therefore puts it on the same level with uncircumcision, which no Jewish or Gentile convert was foolish enough to imagine a means of acceptance with God. In fact, both Jews and Gentiles were condemned by the Divine Law which they had broken, and their only prospect of recovery was through faith in Christ. *A new creation* is the one thing needful to a sinner. A new birth through the power of the Holy Spirit, by which he enters on a life of love, joy, peace, longsuffering, kindness, goodness, fidelity, meekness, self-control, is the only means of justification. And this is *a new creation:* not a shoot from the old sinful nature, but a holy seed implanted by the Spirit of God and nourished by his grace.

16. And as many as walk (or, *shall walk*) **by this rule, peace be on them, and**

17 From henceforth let no man trouble me: for I bear in my body the marks of the Lord Jesus.
18 Brethren, the grace of our Lord Jesus Christ be with your Spirit. Amen.

17 From henceforth let no man trouble me: for I bear branded on my body the marks of Jesus.
18 The grace of our Lord Jesus Christ be with your spirit, brethren. Amen.

mercy, and upon the Israel of God. 'This rule,' or canon, is the principle just stated (ver. 15) that everything depends on a *new creation* in Christ Jesus. And if we adopt the reading 'shall walk,' we see that Paul recognizes the necessity of abiding in the truth and acting in harmony with it. He does not invoke the peace of God upon those that are now walking by this rule, or that have accepted it hitherto, but upon such as continue to the end in such a course. And by 'the Israel of God' he means without doubt the true Israel, those who are sons of God through faith in his Son, whether of Jewish or Gentile descent after the flesh.

17-18. Personal Request and Benediction.

17. From henceforth let no man trouble me. That is, by calling in question my apostolic authority or by perverting my gospel. The words may be literally rendered: *Henceforth let no one prepare for me heavy labors, or troubles.* For Paul was often oppressed by the care of all the churches, and especially when any of them were rent by factions, or were in danger of being led away from the truth. Such conditions imposed heavy burdens on him, filled his spirit with anxiety, and would have been insupportable but for the strength which Christ imparted to him. (Phil. 4:13.) For I bear in my body—or, *For I bear branded on my body the marks of Jesus.*

(Revised Version.) The pronoun 'I' is emphatic, implying that this was not true of Judaizing teachers who had impeached his authority and attempted to render his work vain. Moreover, he appeals to the scars which were in his body as signs of the persecution which he had suffered for Christ's sake, and as brand-marks declaring that he was Christ's bondservant. "The marks attested who the apostle's Master was." (Ellicott.) "Jesus is my Master, my Protector. His brand is stamped on my body. I bear this badge of an honorable service." (Lightfoot.) See John 15:20; 16:2; 2 Tim. 3:12; 2 Cor. 4:10; 11:23.

18. Brethren, the grace of our Lord Jesus Christ, etc. *The grace of our Lord Jesus Christ be with your spirit, brethren. Amen.* (Revised Version.) The only difference between the Common Version and the Revised Version is in the position of the word 'brethren.' In the original it stands at the close of the sentence, "an unusual and emphatic position; compare Philemon 7." "Thus," says Bengel, "the severity of the whole Epistle is softened." Note also the benediction itself, which directs the minds of his readers to 'the grace of our Lord Jesus Christ' as the sum of all good. And then with the ratifying 'Amen' the great apostle commits this wonderful Epistle to some faithful messenger, who will bear it quickly to the churches of Galatia.

www.ingramcontent.com/pod-product-compliance
Lightning Source LLC
Chambersburg PA
CBHW022142090426
42742CB00010B/1359